Tangled Web of Words

A breakthrough guide to Conversational and Coercive Control in relationships

Dr Torna Pitman

Disclaimer

All opinions expressed in the book are entirely the author's. Names have been changed for privacy reasons. All rights reserved. No part of this book may be reproduced by any mechanical, photographic, or electronic process, or in the form of a phonographic recording; nor may it be stored in a retrieval system, transmitted, or otherwise be copied for public or private use other than for "fair use" as brief quotations embodied in articles and reviews without prior written permission of the author and/or publisher.

Cataloguing-in-Publication Data is on file at the Legal Deposit State Library of South Australia and the National Library of Australia.

Ebook ISBN: 13:978-0-6486255-0-6
Paperback ISBN: 13:978-0-6486255-1-3

First Edition, June 2024

Dedicated to

my beloved children, Bonnie Harris and Elo Birkeland.

About the Author

Dr Torna Pitman has dedicated over two decades to the study, research, and practice of addressing Conversational and Coercive Control in interpersonal relationships. With a rich background as a social work academic and counselling practitioner, she has been at the forefront of understanding and combatting this insidious form of manipulation since 2005.

Her groundbreaking PhD research delved deeply into the dynamics of Coercive Control, drawing compelling parallels to an interpersonal colonising process where one partner systematically denies the other autonomy, agency, and equality. This work has been instrumental in illuminating the commonality of tactics used in all forms of abuse and control.

Through her extensive experience teaching practitioners as well as counselling individuals or couples affected by trauma, relationship issues, and family violence, Dr Pitman has refined her theories to emphasise the critical role of conversational dynamics in emotional and psychological abuse as well as Coercive Control. Her seminal article, 'Living with Coercive Control: Trapped within a Complex Web of Double Standards, Double Binds, and Boundary Violations (2017)', has become a key resource for understanding and addressing these complex dynamics.

Recognised internationally for her expertise, Dr. Pitman provides invaluable resources through publicly available materials and videos, helping both professionals and individuals navigate the challenges of Coercive Control. As the Director of TalkingWise, she leads online courses, coaching, and counselling programs that empower individuals to reclaim their agency and break free from abusive relationships.

Dr. Pitman's work continues to make a significant impact in the field, offering hope and practical solutions to those affected by Coercive Control.

Please note: All names and situations have been changed to protect privacy and safety.

Contents

Introduction 1

1. Behind These Pages – My Story 7
2. Lessons from the Tangled Web 13
3. Are We Having a Conversation or a Power Struggle? – A Conversational Framework 19
4. Let's stay in the Middle Column 35
5. How to Respond to Conversational Control 49
6. Higher Levels of Conversational Control – Coercive Control 73
7. Untangling Themes in Conversations 93
8. Untangling Agendas in Conversations 111
9. Why does this matter? 127

Acknowledgements 135
Work with Torna 138
Diagrams and Worksheets 139
Resources 145
Bibliography 147

Introduction

'He was just stubborn, and that was his way. He got what he wanted; he left me with nothing to say. I had to come to terms with the fact that I couldn't win with him. We weren't connected. I might be able to stand up to some things, but then there are a million other things that go beneath the surface, or I just can't quite get the grip of, and it was too hard and too fast to bother with, so I just tried to tread water and not go under. The atmosphere this all created was awful. Why should I have to do this with someone who was supposed to love me and be my partner? His force was *way* stronger than my capacity to make sense of it or stand up to it. It was just a tangled web of words that had me stuck and miserable.'

Karly

This book is about how conversations lead to or prevent Relational Justice. Imagine a relationship where sincere efforts ensured that both people benefited equally. There would be a level playing field, and no one would come off second best in any part of the relationship. It takes good conversations to achieve and then maintain Relational Justice. What Karly experienced was Conversational Control.

Conversational Control is unlikely to be a term you have heard before. Most likely you have experienced it but didn't understand what was happening or couldn't articulate how such a conversation left you feeling. Maybe you sensed something didn't feel right but didn't know what it was or how to address it. At its basis, Conversational Control encompasses all the aspects that can prevent, hinder, complicate, mismanage, derail, or ruin a conversation.

I interviewed Karly for my PhD, which I completed after finishing my degree in Social Work. My PhD outlines the dynamics that make a relationship unjust and unequal, such as in Family Violence. Karly, like most of my research participants and counselling clients, was struggling to make sense of and deal with the impact of how her partner spoke to her and the way the conversations went.

From my data analysis and twenty years of social work practitioner experience, I coined the term Conversational Control in reference to the wide range of unfair tactics used to prevent a conversation from being fair or useful. It is a failure to use conversational manners.

At its best, it is an occasional occurrence with no great consequences for the other person, or it may be more issue-based. Certain conversations go wrong between people, which creates relationship stress, but with proper conversations this can be fixed.

At its worst, like for Karly, it is a relentless conversational pattern that is abusive and creates an imbalance of power. Karly was treated as a second-class citizen. There was no possibility of an equal playing field or Relational Justice. The way her conversations went was typical of an unfair, abusive relationship, and where there is Family Violence and Coercive Control.

Coercive Control is a pattern of relating and behaving used by one person in an intimate relationship to dominate and control another person's life. A high level of Conversational Control is used to train, groom and coerce their partner into submission.

To help us see when a conversation is going wrong, it's good to ask ourselves when a conversation actually works well. What makes it so that it feels good to be in? What creates an outcome where both people feel connected and respected? This is one example of learning conversational dynamics so you can tell when you are being Conversationally Controlled.

I wish Karly had known about Conversational Control, as she would have easily been able to make sense of her partner's tactics and know if and how it was possible to intervene.

This book will help you understand how Conversational Control underlies most relationship issues. It can prevent Relational Justice, whether over the entire relationship or in certain issues or areas. In this book, I explain your Conversational Rights, which we can stand firm on no matter how we are being spoken to.

I show you how to do what Karly couldn't: to disentangle how and why conversations don't work and what to do about it. If Karly had known about this, she would have had the language, clarity, and decision-making power to get the help she needed and stay psychologically independent of her partner's limitations.

For people experiencing a lesser degree of Conversational Control, having this skill will help them retain their dignity and ability to make changes in a current relationship issue. Alternatively, they will be empowered to seek a better one with someone with a greater capacity to relate fairly.

For the last twenty years, as a social work academic, researcher, counsellor, and practitioner, every client I have ever spoken to has realised the effect that Conversational Control has had on them. They saw how difficult it was to make sense of and, therefore, to do anything about it. It made no difference if they were 'clever' people in high places or people who felt they were barely getting by.

An important point is that Conversational Control is everywhere in society, especially within intimate relationships, to varying degrees. Whatever level we experience will result in an unhealthy dynamic where some, too many, or maybe all conversations make us feel unheard and disconnected from a person.

We can all use Conversational Control at times simply because we are human, and our conversations are not always sanitised and perfect! However, the difference lies in whether it is a pattern of

Conversational Control that puts the other person at a disadvantage or disrupts the connection. Does the level of Conversational Control make the relationship unjust in some way? Has it prevented an equal playing field?

Some people I work with worry whether they are using Conversational Control. We all use it occasionally out of exasperation, distress, or anger. We can react and speak before thinking. Throughout the world, and throughout history, we have lacked role modelling for healthy conversations. However, once we fully understand Conversational Control, it's much easier to know whether our conversational slip-ups create a scene, a rupture, or prevent an equal playing field. We also know what to do about it.

Becoming aware of how we communicate and understanding what makes a conversation work is the key for both parties to achieve positive outcomes.

Tangled Web of Words— A breakthrough guide to Conversational and Coercive Control in relationships can guide you, whether you are trying to make sense of a current or past relationship, or feeling concerned about entering a new one.

Once I outline the Conversational Control Framework I have developed, you will know what to look for. It will be clear to you when a conversation has gone outside the safe, workable zone, which I call The Middle Column. You won't be available to take an accommodating, adjusting, or conforming role to someone's level of Conversational Control. Instead, you'll keep your identity and autonomy, and know what's best for you.

By the time you finish reading all the chapters in this book, you will understand the Conversational Control Framework. This means you will be able to:

1. Understand your Conversational Rights.
2. Spot Unfair Conversational Control tactics.

3. Recognise conversations that create or prevent Relational Justice.
4. Identify when a conversation is in or out of the Middle Column.
5. Have the framework and phrases to use when a conversation is outside the Middle Column.
6. Have the clarity and skills to make sense of any Tangled Web of Words you encounter.

As a guide to using this book, I recommend reading it all through first to understand the Conversational Control Framework. Then, go back and study the framework and phrases more closely so you know what to do and say.

Having a framework and the skills to navigate your way through Conversational Control is life-changing.

Disclaimer
Individuals experiencing higher levels of Conversational Control or Coercive Control should only employ any of the strategies in this book if they feel safe to do so, preferably with the guidance of a professional. Sometimes, it is safer to cater or submit rather than risk retaliation. It is better to stay safe. Living with someone with a superior, entitled and adversarial attitudinal style means you can expect retaliation should you stand up for yourself or call them out. Please talk to someone you trust or reach out to professionals who can help you. I have listed trusted resources at the back of this book. You are not alone.

1

Behind These Pages – My Story

How did I find myself on this journey?

It began with feeling the impact, as a child, of conversations disconnecting me from other people, and the loneliness and sadness that come with that. As an older adult, I have the words and concepts to understand why conversations with so many people in my life often felt difficult, like they left me high and dry, unheard, as if I didn't matter or that everything was somehow my fault. As a child, I couldn't have articulated that at all.

As I grew up, I watched and observed women being silenced by men, girls bullying each other, and words used in ways that made people sad and unmotivated. I saw this everywhere and between any age or gender. I was devasted to see people desperately wanting to be heard and responded to. I didn't understand why they weren't.

Family

At nine years of age, I told my grandmother off several times about how she was talking to my step-grandfather. He couldn't look after himself that well; he was older than her, disabled, and struggled to walk. One night, she jeered at him about what he would do if she and I went out and left him to fend for himself. I watched his face and demeanour droop as he sat there eating his dinner, and it broke my heart. I was mortified and very sorry for him. I couldn't believe my grandmother spoke so differently to everyone else. Mustering my courage, I told her to stop treating him like that. She was shocked and furious. I eventually lost trust in her after several incidents like this where she scolded and scorned him, and I'd tell her to stop. I knew I made her angry, and she told me as a teenager that she nearly slapped my face. I was wary of her.

For some unknown reason, I focused on how people spoke to one another in any relationship. In the classroom, though, I had my first glimpse of standing up to someone in authority about the profound impact of their words.

School

I vividly remember a certain event in primary school. I was a good student and used schoolwork and the routine to offset my home life. At the onset of fifth grade, I was just eleven years old, and I faced a formidable teacher with striking purple hair and piercing blue eyes—Mrs B. She was renowned for her strict and uncompromising demeanour, and I was petrified of being in her classroom.

Not long after term one started, my world was shaken when I failed to hear her command to put our pencils down because I was so engrossed in my work. To my shock, Mrs B subjected me to a loud and public accusation in front of the whole class, which included all fifth and sixth-grade pupils. As a fifth-grade student, we really looked up to the sixth graders! So being publicly called out was even worse in front of them.

'Torna Pitman, you are either deaf or disobedient. Get up and go and stand in the cloakroom until I call you back in.'

I remember the strange buzz in my head and the feeling of having ice-cold water thrown at me. As if humiliating me with words wasn't enough, I had to get up and do a walk of shame from the front of the class to the back, to the door of the frigid cloakroom. The experience initially left me feeling deeply ashamed and shocked. I wondered if maybe I was a bit deaf, or was it because I was disobedient? This felt confusing as I was always too scared at school to be remotely disobedient. And if I was a bit deaf, wasn't she being mean about that? I grappled so hard with this dilemma for days, and I was in a state of high anxiety. Out of nowhere, though, I started to feel angry and indignant. My instincts told me something was amiss in her accusations.

I finally worked it out that being told I was either this thing (deaf) or that thing (disobedient), and both are bad, was unfair. I know now that Mrs B had used a Double Bind confining me to two demeaning options. She tried to humiliate me by putting me in a no-win situation. I decided that I would politely let her know. It's not like I had good role modelling at home to compare Mrs B with; I just seemed to have this radar for, and an objection to, unfair conversations.

I composed a passionate letter to Mrs B, asserting that I was neither deaf nor disobedient. My explanation was straightforward: I had been focusing hard on my work and hadn't heard her instructions. I apologised and clarified that I had come to school to learn and did not want to waste my time confined to a freezing cloakroom 'where one does not learn academic subjects!' I still have that letter.

To my surprise, Mrs B, the stern figure I had feared, became an unexpected friend who supported me wholeheartedly. Despite our rough start, she was someone who helped me to feel good about myself! Some people respond well when they are politely countered or challenged, but others, of course, will not.

Teaching

It was almost inevitable that I would become a qualified teacher. I loved creating a positive, happy classroom environment where learning could flourish without harsh words, putdowns, or fear.

Yet I grappled with the realisation that my skills were sometimes insufficient. Teaching was just one facet of conversing with students. I wanted to delve deeper to better understand the conversational skills needed to connect with them. After all, they were not merely students but unique individuals with their own needs, concerns, and challenges.

This realisation reached a crisis point for me during a school camp with Grade Eleven and Twelve students. I found myself seated on a couch between two young male students, and each started to share their experiences of sexual abuse simultaneously. They both seemed totally unaware that the other was also talking with me. I am unsure if they could hear each other (there was a lot of noise in the room) or if they simply didn't care because they needed to talk. I was profoundly moved and shaken by their revelations. The sexual abuse they had experienced, which included being kidnapped, meant that as well as the trauma of this never being addressed in their lives, these beautiful young men had faced significant struggles within the education system and had fallen between the cracks.

This pivotal moment marked a turning point in my journey. As much as I loved teaching, I wanted to learn about ways to connect on a deeper level and to have conversations that mattered and were helpful.

Counselling

To gain the skills I lacked, I decided to study counselling. While counselling provided valuable insights and tools, in those days it primarily focused on an individual's coping skills. I transitioned into a social work degree, where I learned about the various social, political, and legal influences that shape our lives. Throughout my social work study and training, I began to understand certain patterns of communication that led to domination.

These patterns informed me of the dynamics of power, control, and manipulation within relationships. I focused on how the words we chose, the tones we adopted, and even the silences we maintained played pivotal roles in shaping our communication's effectiveness and impact on others.

Research and Clients

At the end of my social work degree, I started work as a relationship counsellor and, at the same time, was given a scholarship to complete a PhD. My first PhD topic was forgiveness!

Many of my clients were women and children petrified of contact with their ex-partner/father. There was a lack of understanding in those days of how family violence was far more than physical abuse. Rather, it is a whole course of conduct that is hostile, controlling and dominating. Yet these women and children were treated as if they were the problem, and all eyes were on the mother as to whether she was alienating the father from the children, rather than the behaviour of the father pre- and post-separation. It is a shocking situation for any mother and child to be in. I was fast losing interest in forgiveness.

They were hurt, confused, sometimes devastated, and traumatised by the nature of the conversations in their intimate relationships or with people they loved, but there was no easy way to describe this, so how could there be any focus on forgiveness? I became acutely aware that the pain and turmoil within their relationships often centred around words. This included the conversations that took place and became tangled, and the conversations that never occurred or should have happened.

I wanted to know far more about this area in order to articulate it. Forgiveness can only be authentic and useful once we know exactly what we're forgiving and its impact on us. Otherwise, it is premature, destructive and misses the point.

I changed my PhD topic from forgiveness to a focus on relationship dynamics, particularly how they worked in unequal relationships including Domestic/Family Violence and Coercive Control. My supervisor was disappointed. Domestic Violence was not a popular topic, and it was usually seen as physical violence. In 2005, Coercive Control was still mysterious and unknown.

But I was adamant I wanted to do something about the terrible injustices I witnessed in my practice.

2

Lessons from the Tangled Web

I had the privilege of interviewing and engaging deeply with participants who generously shared their experiences of abusive relationships. Their stories highlighted not only the conduct their partners and ex-partners subjected them to but also their impossible conversational style. They described conversations that were twisted, hurtful, shut down, or refused and how this rendered their relationships unworkable and devastating. The consequences were far-reaching, resulting in emotional scars and a loss of psychological and material independence.

Jan's Story – Low-level Conversational Control

Jan was a counselling client. She was relatively happy in her relationship with John, but she felt affected because John would not talk about several issues. He had many ways to avoid, prevent, shut down, or ruin a conversation around two topics: labour division and parenting. Jan was distressed about her overload of responsibility when it came to running the house and looking after the children. They both worked part-time, and enjoyed a nice social life. However, Jan was bursting with resentment at being unable to engage John in a useful conversation about how they could divide household and parenting tasks so that she felt less tired and stressed, and had more time for herself.

John had some pretty good tactics. He would get grumpy, or morose, or tell her things were fine as they were, or that she needed to be more efficient. Jan became reluctant to raise the issues because of the inevitable let down when John would evade, deny, or complicate the issue rather than address it. Finally, she learnt what tactics he was using to control the conversations and what she could do to counter him. She no longer felt hesitant in approaching him in case he got grumpy or morose. Jan refused to be Conversationally Controlled.

Hazel's Story – High-Level Conversational Control

One research participant who profoundly impacted me was Hazel She endured years in a marriage where her partner skilfully controlled their conversations. He dictated the discussion topics, how conversations unfolded, and when they would end. Hazel felt voiceless as her opinions, feelings, and needs were brushed aside. She longed to express herself but couldn't quite grasp how the power dynamics within their conversations had eroded her voice.

Her partner used Conversational Control tactics to convince her he was right, leading her to believe she 'just didn't understand' and 'you just won't let me love you'. Hazel wished she recognised the signs of Conversational Control earlier. She had descended into confusion and depression.

Instead of focusing on the nature of their conversations and how he controlled them, she turned inward, reflecting on herself and her upbringing. Hazel was unsure if her relationship was abusive and had been told by other practitioners it wasn't. She was in therapy for her relationship with her mother. It wasn't until she untangled the conversational patterns with her partner that she realised he had trained her over time to defer to him. Once she realised this, she also noticed how she was being controlled by other non-conversational tactics to ensure the relationship met his needs and never hers.

The level of abuse in her relationship was at the high end of the Conversational Control continuum. This, and a dominating behavioural style, is Coercive Control.

David's Story – Conversational Grooming

If the type of Conversational Control being used is systematically aimed at making you useful rather than equal, it is Conversational Grooming. In other words, there is a pattern and system of Conversational Control tactics to achieve unfair and undue influence over you.

David was another research participant who left an indelible mark on me. His husband had conversationally groomed him into surrendering control of the family's finances. What seemed an innocent process evolved into a situation where David was skilfully kept in the dark about their economic status. Unbeknown to him, he had relinquished his financial independence.

David's husband used Conversational Tactics that were not always obvious, loud, or overbearing. They were quiet and seductive. His experiences were a stark reminder that influencing someone can be done without resorting to overtly impolite or forceful Conversational Tactics. Conversational Grooming can be a less obvious, subtle use of Conversational Control to prepare someone to be compliant and amenable without them even knowing about it.

For example, David's husband was always pleasant, charming, and friendly. He would say to David, 'I know how busy you are, let me organise the money as I think I find that less taxing than you.' Or, 'Goodness, you are spending quite a lot lately on clothes, let's pull back a little so we can go on holiday this Christmas.' He was so pleasant about it that David would squirm with embarrassment and pull back obediently. He didn't realise until far too late that his husband had been graciously steering the conversations in his favour whilst he was spending what he liked and skilfully avoiding proper conversations about their financial arrangements. In the end, this really cost David as his husband fleeced him.

Back to Karly's Story

As Karly tried to make sense of her situation, she told me:

> 'We rarely even had discussions because, in the end, I just wouldn't discuss or even argue the point. He wouldn't have seen reason in what I had to say, so it didn't matter; there was just no point, and there still is no point because he still doesn't see that he was ever in the wrong.
>
> He would just come home and not talk to me. He would freeze me out and not acknowledge me as being there at all, at times, and then I was trying to work out all the things I might have done that week to see if I had done something to cause that reaction. Whenever I tried to ask, 'Why are you doing this?' there would be no answer, no apology, no discussion, no negotiation.
>
> Sometimes, he would 'get at' me and start criticising, demanding, and telling me who I was and wasn't. I would do anything to avoid bringing that on. I think he probably didn't like me to challenge him. You know, he'd use those looks, snarls, and tone of voice. I used to hate the feelings they would create in me, like fear and rejection. I'd feel so insignificant. It could be like talking to a wall...He didn't hear or take in anything I said and respond to it properly.
>
> I felt like I was fading away. I even knew I couldn't talk to him about that. I'd have been fobbed off. 'Don't be so dramatic; you're exaggerating, what a stupid thing to say,' or something like that. I'd be accused, and then it would be turned back on me; 'What about you? You do this...What about when you...?'
>
> He would never answer me without accusing me. No matter how I tried to put it into words, it was like, 'I don't even know what you're talking about.' I'd go away wondering how I got it so wrong.

It's so confusing because it's not like all the attacks were coming nicely in a row. It is more like they come every which way, and you don't know which way to defend yourself.'

At this level, the relationship is saturated in Conversational Control. She had no equal say in any part of the relationship, for example, in the financial or social arrangements, the sexual relationship, the division of labour, or the parenting roles.

As Karly said, she did not have the knowledge or understanding to make sense of it or stand up to it. She wondered, instead, what was wrong with her and became sad, confused, lonely, depressed, and anxious.

What Do These Stories Say?

These stories and countless others helped me create theories of relationship dynamics and how a relationship can tilt from fair to coercive through Conversational Control and Conversational Grooming. I felt like I stumbled upon a hidden realm, a world where seemingly ordinary conversations could cause significant harm or be integrated into a pattern of grooming and control.

Conversations mould, influence, and transform individuals and relationships. If someone you are close to, like an intimate partner, friend, or relative, has a pattern of relating to you in a conversationally controlling manner, it is a betrayal. After all, they are supposed to have your best interests at heart. But when their conversational style causes you to come off second-best, this creates much grief and loss.

My clients and research participants taught me not only how Conversational Control can work at the lower end and include a Conversational Grooming process in the higher end, but also how hard it is to make sense of and process that. They taught me that it can happen to anybody from any socioeconomic background, race, religion, family of origin, gender, age, intelligence, or experience.

Conversational Control is used worldwide to gain and maintain control over individuals, groups, and countries. Whatever you do, do not make the mistake of thinking it is about you. It is a feature of the human condition to use Conversational Control to gain and maintain the upper hand in any situation.

3

Are We Having a Conversation or a Power Struggle? – A Conversational Framework

After all these years of researching, studying, teaching, and counselling, I couldn't help but notice that many of the issues I heard about came from people mishandling or avoiding conversations. This led me to develop the Conversational Control Framework I am now outlining for you.

How we communicate with one another – the sorts of conversations that we are good at and the ones that we can't or won't have – play a huge role in how our relationships feel. For example, you may be in an intimate relationship or a friendship with someone who uses Unfair Conversational Tactics to discuss topics that you are capable of discussing fairly and healthily. This is a difficult situation to be in.

Grasping the concepts in this book may offer insight and hope for any confusing, unsatisfying, or unsafe relationships you have experienced or are currently worried about.

But first, why do conversations matter?

Attitude

Talking is the main form of communication between people; we talk with our attitude, body language, and actual words. Many people don't recognise the effect of their attitude when speaking, and some purposely use a contemptuous or hostile attitude to control conversations and have the effect they want.

We convey our attitude through the subtle set of our muscles, how we move, sit or stand, and the expressions on our faces. It's possible to convey what we think about a person with minimal effort, even just by sitting there and staring into space instead of talking.

If someone wants to control a conversation, they can do it just with an attitude. Imagine trying to talk to someone whose attitude towards you conveys disinterest. We can pick up on someone's attitude towards us without there being any observable body language. It is the 'energy' or vibe that someone gives off, whether they are sitting still or doing something.

Body Language and Facial Expressions

Let's think about everything we do with our body when we speak, including the tone of our voice. I watch for things like how people's gestures work, whether they are open or intimidating, whether they get too close, what their facial expressions are like, whether their teeth are gritted, and if their eyes are hard. Is their body language distracted? Do they look at their phone, turn away, act bored, disappear out of the room, or refuse to respond? What are they doing while they are talking to you? All these things convey so much in a conversation.

A person who wants to control the conversation will consciously notice when your attitude and body language show you are uncertain, and will use that to press their point. This can all happen outside of our conscious awareness, but a controlling person will use this tactic consciously to ensure that every conversation goes their way and their way only.

In any relationship, a combination of attitude, body language and facial expressions can be used instead of words to threaten the other person into silence and submission.

It is true that there are cultural differences in how we convey disrespect through attitude, body language, and facial expressions. Eye contact, for example, is encouraged in some cultures but not in others. While it is important to take this into account as well for healthy communication, clear disrespect should never be dismissed with this excuse.

The Spoken Word

If we add spoken words, we have even more communication happening.

Someone's communication can range from listening to you and asking good questions to controlling the conversation. For example, by:

- monopolising it
- interrupting
- blaming
- shaming
- interrogating
- accusing
- deflecting
- evading the issue
- changing the topic
- refusing to join the conversation altogether

When Conversational Control happens regularly in any relationship, it undermines trust and is hurtful. Dismissing or overriding someone's input creates frustration, resentment, and distance. It can happen occasionally without long-lasting consequences, but the relationship can't grow or develop when there are too many poorly handled conversations. It tilts from a relationship that may have once been healthy to one that deteriorates.

Introducing 'A Continuum' of Conversational Control in Relationships

Picture your relationships existing on a sliding scale. You have the ideal at one end–relationships filled with respect, open communication, and a sense of equality. Both people feel free to express themselves and make decisions. It's a place of balance and harmony. Isn't that what we all want?

However, as you move along the scale, you may encounter something entirely different. This is where control creeps in. Conversations shift, and decisions become one-sided. One person starts dominating, often at the expense of the other's happiness and freedom.

I want you to understand that it's normal for relationships to encounter challenges or conflicts. These are opportunities for growth and understanding. However, it's crucial to recognise when the balance tips toward control. This is where things can go awry.

Tactics Used in Conversational Control – Arcing Up and Arcing Down

Now, let's break down what I mean by Conversational Control.

A person practicing Conversational Control uses two key types of tactics in conversations to get you to defer to them: Arcing Up and Arcing Down, as you can see in the table below. They overlap a little; it's not a concrete split. It's more about how someone uses the tactics that is different.

In the framework I have developed, there are three columns: The Arcing Down Column, the Arcing Up Column, and the Middle Column. The below table shows some of the attitudes, body language signals, and verbal tactics that can be used when people Arc Up and Arc Down rather than use the Middle Column.

The Arcing Down Column

Attitude

- Indifference
- Distracted
- Depressed
- Vulnerable
- Bored
- Oppositional
- Poor me
- Self pity
- Morose

Use of body

- Slumps, sighs
- Eye rolls
- Sulks, cries
- Leaves the room
- Shoulder shrugs
- Mumbles/mutters
- Distracts with TV, phone
- Looks away
- Fiddles, ignores

Spoken Word

- Evasive, confusing
- Refuses to engage
- Denies the problem
- Defensive
- Pretends to go along
- Changes the topic
- Withholds information

The Middle Column

IT'S A WIN/WIN

✓ Allows for emotional connection, teamwork, and maturity

✓ Promotes safety, fairness, and equal voice in decisions

✓ Enables growth and evolution of the relationship

The Arcing Up Column

Attitude

- Contemptuous
- Snide
- Secretive
- Fault-finding
- Unempathic
- Hostile
- Dismissive
- Disapproving
- Infantilising

Use of body

- Comes too close
- Hands on hips
- Menacing facial expressions
- Gritted teeth
- Snarling
- Glaring
- Unsettling vocal intonations
- Punching walls

Spoken Word

- Blames, shames, defames
- Distorts
- Deflects
- Gaslights
- Name-calls
- Point-scores
- Commands
- Mocks
- Ridicules

Diagram 1-The Three Columns

A person who tends to control conversations with their partner, either occasionally or constantly, moves between Arcing Down and Arcing Up tactics very quickly and randomly, and it is difficult to keep up with what is going on. The confusion is a part of the control. They will avoid the Middle Column.

An essential thing to remember is that if we are in a relationship with someone with a habit of controlling some or all of the conversations, they will have a pattern of Arcing Up or Down. Some people swap between the two very quickly and suddenly, yet others tend to use more Arcing Up tactics than Arcing Down tactics. Everyone is different.

The Arcing Down Column

This is an important group of tactics where they go down the victim route to get you to cater and defer to how disappointed or distressed they are. They are not 'with you'; they have 'turned away from you' with the idea that you will turn towards their needs at your expense.

Using Arcing Down, they unconsciously or consciously aim to make you feel worried and have a degree of fear, inferiority, obligation, guilt, shame, or confusion. When we feel these things, we are prone to being more amenable, giving in and deferring. We tend to go into a response cycle where we are led by the tactic they are using and we respond from the back foot. This means the Arcing Down tactic was successful.

The Arcing Up Column

The other group of equally important tactics is where they 'turn against you' to get you to submit, and defer to how disapproving, right through to disgusted, they are. They are not 'with you'; they are against you with the idea that you will give in to their way of seeing things.

When someone uses Arcing Up, they unfairly want you to submit to them by making you feel the same emotions that Arcing Down elicits, such as fear. Again, you will tend to go into a response cycle where their tactics govern the conversation as you are being led and controlled.

The Middle Column

This is where a conversation will work because no tactics are being used, and the mutual aim is to create emotional safety, respect, and connection.

When somebody is 'with you' in a conversation, they are trying to direct the conversation in a way that meets both your perspectives and needs. This is when you know that something can be sorted out, even if it takes a while, and that nobody will subject you to Unfair Conversational Tactics like Arcing Up and Arcing Down. You are emotionally and psychologically safe.

Being in the 'Middle Column' allows real connection and friendship, whether in an intimate relationship, with a relative, or with a friend. This means you have a happy relationship where you love talking with them because they will listen, and you feel heard, at least most of the time. You can say what you feel without repercussions.

Which Unfair Conversational Tactics Trigger You?

We tend to be triggered by some Unfair Conversational Tactics more than others, but we may be unaware of it and try to make sense of what is happening in other ways. For example, we might think we are just feeling sensitive or having a bad day. But sometimes we are triggered by, and therefore reactive to, particular combinations of attitude, body language, tone, and words, but not others.

Some of us are entirely silenced by any or just some of the tactics that convey disapproval or disgust (Arcing Up), so we submit. Some of us are prone to catering to an important person in our life who uses certain Arcing Down tactics because we can't stand seeing them distressed or disappointed, no matter how unfair it is when we consider the bigger picture.

This is all very common, but when it gets out of hand, it will drive a wedge in the relationship and tip it into being unequal and maybe abusive. It depends on the cunning of the person using Unfair Conversational Tactics, such as purposefully and unfairly acting distressed or disappointed to make you cater to them, knowing full well that this will be to your disadvantage.

Meet Jesse

Jesse was in a relationship with Kai. Jesse really struggled when Kai Arced Up but was not so affected when Kai Arced Down. An Arcing Up tactic that Jesse was most sensitive to was when Kai had a superior attitude, used hostile body language and facial expressions (hands on hips, setting their jaw, and glaring) and verbally blamed Jesse for the issue Jesse was trying to discuss. Jesse immediately felt anxiety, confusion, and guilt because of Kai's disapproval. They couldn't think straight and became ungrounded. Yet, when Kai used any of the Arcing Down Tactics in response to a conversation, Jesse was more likely to stay grounded. This means they will not play into Kai's attempts to get them to cater.

We all have different strengths and difficulties with certain types of Unfair Conversational Tactics. To some extent, it can depend upon the skills we developed or weren't able to develop in our family of origin, through relatives, or at school. It can be influenced by the different areas of our lives where we have been overwhelmed, hurt, or traumatised by how we were spoken to. But in the end, no matter why, we are all susceptible to feeling anxious, confused, obligated, guilty or shamed when someone refuses to use fair conversation. It is part and parcel of how we have always communicated. Conversations and words can be weapons that sear our souls and leave us traumatised, or they can be a vital and healing form of communication.

Unfortunately, humans instinctively know how to use Conversational Control to get their way. It doesn't necessarily mean that someone is a 'bad person', but it means they may be poor, unsafe, and unkind communicators. When someone has already reaped the benefits of using Conversational Control, they have noticed what makes certain people, such as you, easier to control. They will use that information to get you to cater to their Arcing Down or submit to their Arcing Up so that you gradually give away your power. Healthy communicators, however, will be cautious of leaving the Middle Column to ensure conversations work.

Window of Tolerance

When we are in our Window of Tolerance, we can think clearly, we know what we are feeling, and we can make decisions. Being grounded and regulated means we are in the Window of Tolerance, and our nervous system is balanced.

Conversational Control can put us out of our Window of Tolerance by triggering us so that we can't think clearly, and it feels impossible to be regulated or stay calm. We are unable to stand up for ourselves from a place of power. A person wanting to control a conversation will purposely put us out of our Window of Tolerance so that we are no longer able to process information and decide on a response from a more regulated space. We can have different trauma responses to Arcing Up and Arcing Down tactics.

4 Types of Trauma Responses:

There are four main types of trauma responses: Fight, Flight, Freeze and Fawn. You may find yourself reacting to someone using tactics of Conversational Control towards you in the following ways:

1. **Fight-Angry**
   We feel angry and can find ourselves becoming argumentative, talking back, bristling or blowing up, being irritable, mean, yelling, quarrelsome, paying them back, or loudly defending our honour.

2. **Flight-Anxious**
   We feel nervous and want to flee the situation or anxiously defend ourselves from what they are saying. We vainly try to justify, argue, defend, or explain and are desperate for reassurance or connection.

3. **Freeze-Shocked**
   We are paralysed, can clam up, feel dissociated, immobilised, and unable to respond. We can't even think, let alone respond.

4. **Fawn-Appeasing**
   We respond by placating, trying to please, trying to make it right, and over-giving.

Certain combinations of attitudes, body language and verbal tactics trigger our pattern of trauma response. If trauma reactions are a big part of the relationship you have with someone, there is something wrong as your nervous system is responding on an emotional and psychological as well as a physical level to threats to your safety.

Be aware. Some people who use Conversational Control will accuse you of causing their Arcing Up or Arcing Down and say they were merely trauma reactions. You will notice that some of the examples of how we respond when having a trauma reaction are the same as some of the tactics.

The difference between a trauma response and a tactic is that a trauma response is in reaction to being treated unfairly in the first place, not part of a pattern of Arcing Up or Down to control the conversation.

The more you understand how Conversational Control works, the fewer trauma reactions you have; they are not as strong and the quicker you can recover from them.

Below is a diagram that shows the difference between safe and unsafe zones for conversations in terms of trauma responses and Relational Justice.

ARCING DOWN COLUMN Unsafe Zone	MIDDLE COLUMN Safe Zone	ARCING UP COLUMN Unsafe Zone
Tactics used to make you cater to their disappointment or distress	No tactics are employed	Tactics used to make you submit to their disapproval or disgust
• No emotional intimacy	• Emotional connection	• No emotional intimacy
Possible Trauma Reaction • Fight: angry - argue back hotly • Flight: anxious - defend yourself • Freeze: shocked/resigned - can't think what to do or say • Fawn: placate/try to please	Relaxed, Emotionally and Psychologically Safe	**Possible Trauma Reactions** • Fight: angry - argue back hotly • Flight: anxious - defend yourself • Freeze: shocked/resigned - can't think what to do or say • Fawn: placate/try to please
Relational Injustice	**Relational Justice**	**Relational Injustice**

Diagram 2 - Safe and Unsafe Zones

Conversational Control can happen in any part of a relationship: for example, in the financial, social, or sexual domains, how labour and roles are divided, or parenting arrangements. Where it feels like part or all of the relationship is unfair or unequal, it's because the conversations have been outside the Middle Column in some way. This diagram points out how the Middle Column is safe; creates Relational Justice and we do not get stuck in trauma reactions.

Remember, it's helpful to think about Conversational Control in intimate relationships as a continuum ranging from occasionally irritating on the one end to constantly challenging and highly abusive on the other end. The degree of Conversational Control determines where the relationship is placed on that continuum. If someone experiences Coercive Control, for instance, which is on the highly abusive end of the continuum, their partner will constantly use Conversational Control tactics rather than have fair and reasonable conversations.

Meet Sarah and Mark

They've been together for a while, and like any couple, they have their ups and downs. Here's how Arcing Up and Arcing Down happened in their relationship:

Mark had trouble talking about the finances. He earned a full-time wage, and Sarah was at home with the children. What happened when they talked about money was entirely predictable. Sarah told me in counselling that Mark would 'act funny' if she pressed him for information about their budget and talked about how much she needed to run the household successfully. When I asked her what happened when he was 'acting funny', she described it as Mark becoming withdrawn from the conversation she wanted. His attitude would be 'poor me', and his body language distracted. He would fiddle with things, slump his shoulders, or even leave the room. Sarah was aware that the children watched how they spoke with one another.

Mark couldn't stay in the conversation and be with Sarah; he kept emotionally and physically disappearing. He Arced Down and wanted Sarah to back off and cater to his distress at talking about money. Sarah told me she would back off and try to pacify him because she hated to see him in any way distressed or disappointed by her. However, she was hurt and confused by his reaction. It meant the conversations couldn't work, and their finances remained undiscussed, leaving Sarah voiceless and wondering what she was doing wrong.

There were also times when she tried to talk about money and Mark glared at her; his attitude was adversarial, his body language and voice intonation menacing. His choice of words was to interrogate her over what she was spending. He showed anger at her for not being able to stick to the budget he set. He Arced Up and expected Sarah to defer by submitting. She hated his disapproval and would submit to avoid it, especially when the children were around.

They were never in the Middle Column over the finances, causing a rift in their relationship. Sarah was unhappy that there was not enough money to let the children play a sport, learn a musical instrument, or have some pocket money. Mark switched between different Arcing Up and Arcing Down tactics, sometimes so fast that Sarah was constantly on the back foot trying to keep up.

Further, when she didn't respond to his sexual advances in the way he thought she should, Mark would turn away from Sarah, act crushed and disappointed, and say, 'Oh no, not again,' in a very 'poor me', self-pitying tone. Sarah would immediately feel guilty and cater to him by saying, 'I've really had a hard day, maybe tomorrow.'

Suddenly, Mark would Arc Up by raising his voice, glaring at her, and using sarcasm: 'Oh yeah, like last time. What's wrong with you!' Just these two tactics are hard to keep up with and process. But add some complexity, such as Mark switching from sarcasm back to a different Arcing Down tactic such as self-pity: 'After everything I do for this family, I may as well give up.' Mark completely missed the point and the Middle Column. And Sarah was lost in a quagmire of guilt, shame, and confusion.

Sarah didn't realise this was Conversational Control, which put her at a considerable financial disadvantage, otherwise known as financial abuse.

What Mark could not understand was that their sexual relationship was also suffering because of his Conversational Control. Where someone is routinely treated with indifference or intimidation in any area of the relationship, it will show up in other areas, especially the bedroom. Sarah didn't realise she had stopped feeling loved and safe. Mark used various Arcing Up and Down tactics to get Sarah to want to have sex with him, but again, their conversations about sex were never in the Middle Column, and Sarah was suffering. Their relationship stopped working, and they had different ideas about why.

Mark thought:

- Sarah spent too much.
- She wouldn't keep to the budget that he had set.
- He wasn't getting enough sex.
- Sarah wasn't fun in bed any longer.
- He was working five days a week to provide for them all.

Sarah thought:

- Mark was impossible, even unpleasant, to talk with.
- He wouldn't listen to her.
- She could not feel sexually attracted to someone who wasn't listening or responding to her.
- She felt guilty about not wanting sex yet trapped as there were no fair conversations.
- She and the children were not doing well on Mark's budgeting, and it wasn't fair.

Their relationship tilted to accommodate what Mark could talk about, what he refused to or avoided talking about, and what he thought should happen in a relationship. He controlled the conversations but had no conscious awareness of or empathy for the effects this was having on Sarah. She was thrown around and occasionally had a trauma reaction to his Arcing Up and Arcing Down tactics and spent far too much time feeling anxious, obligated, shamed, guilty, or confused. Sarah and Mark had lost sight of the bigger picture and were heading for a breakup.

Many relationships fail exactly because of what was happening in Mark and Sarah's relationship. If the controlling partner can't make amends or doesn't have empathy for all the times their partner doesn't have a say when their life and choices are affected, the relationship can never work.

If they both understood Conversational Control, how to stay in the Middle Column, and what would happen if they didn't, Mark and Sarah would have a framework to help them and to role-model for their children. The way they were talking or not talking about issues was also going to be something the children watched.

I'm reminded of a story I once heard, where the children in the family were never worried or anxious about Mum and Dad arguing because they knew there was no threat and that they always resolved things. Their mother and father were friends and had an instinctive desire to stay in or return to the Middle Column, as anything else was a power struggle and a waste of time.

You might remember a time (or several) when you tried to talk to your partner about something important to you. They may have either Arced Up or Arced Down as a response, and you felt that it wouldn't have taken that much to resolve things and connect more deeply. It hurts and is disconnecting. What makes it worse is if there is a pattern of Conversational Control, such as certain things you cannot ask or particular conversations you can't have to keep the peace. There are 'undiscussables' in the relationship that create a rift. Not enough time is spent in the Middle Column to ensure the relationship is working for both of you and is not meeting one person's needs more than the other.

We need fair conversations for any relationship to feel okay and for both people to flourish. A critical life skill is knowing where this is possible with someone and where it isn't, and avoiding relationships with those who do not intend or understand how to create an equal relationship where the Middle Column is always used.

Once you are familiar with the terms and the sorts of attitudes, body language and verbal tactics that are part of Arcing Up and Arcing Down, it is easier to stay grounded, not get lost in the power struggle, effectively counter the tactics, and invite the person using them into the Middle Column.

Conversational Control happens everywhere. No matter the type of relationship—a friendship, a colleague, a relative, or someone providing us with a service—the use of Conversational Control is upsetting and disempowering. Let's think about an intimate relationship where so much of us is invested in it working well, affecting us on every level. The level of Conversational Control is critical to recognise and know how to respond to. When you have knowledge and awareness, you can make a change.

4

Let's stay in the Middle Column

What if we learned from a young age that no matter how great a relationship initially feels, it won't work well or feel safe and equal when there is not enough time spent in the Middle Column? We would know that the inevitable areas of tension that develop will not have to erode connection and well-being.

When I was growing up in the 1960s and 1970s, there was no focus or information on emotional abuse, psychological abuse, bullying, or controlling and narcissistic behaviours. I am sure I was not the only one who did not do well with bullies, whatever package they came in. Bullying was poorly understood: what it meant, how it looked, and what to do about it. All we seemed to be able to do as a society was focus on physical abuse; when, what type, and in what sort of relationship it was a chargeable offence. What happened in a relationship of any kind, apart from major incidents of physical abuse such as hitting, punching, kicking, and slapping, didn't register. Patterns of less obvious micro-aggressions went unnoticed.

As in Sarah's and Mark's relationship, the finer details of what was happening between them, emotionally, psychologically, and in their conversations, had gone unrecognised and unaddressed.

A Continuum of Conversational Control in relation to the Middle Column

As mentioned previously, thinking of a continuum of Conversational Control is helpful. As you can see in the diagram below, it is more irritating than damaging on the one end of the continuum, and it is more temporary or occasional. For example, two people who occasionally use Unfair Conversational Tactics with one another, but it is of no real long-lasting consequence. Most of their relating is in the Middle Column, so they have a high degree of goodwill and emotional and psychological safety. That is the key. Even so, lower-level Conversational Control can accumulate over time and feel increasingly unmanageable.

The further along the continuum, the less goodwill or emotional and psychological safety there is in the relationship, and the less intention there is to use or stay in the Middle Column. Instead, there is an increasing level of intention to control, influence and make use of the other person. At the highest end of the continuum, we have Coercive Control, the dangerous attitudinal and behavioural pattern at the core of Family Violence.

This diagram will help you understand the different levels along the continuum of Conversational Control.

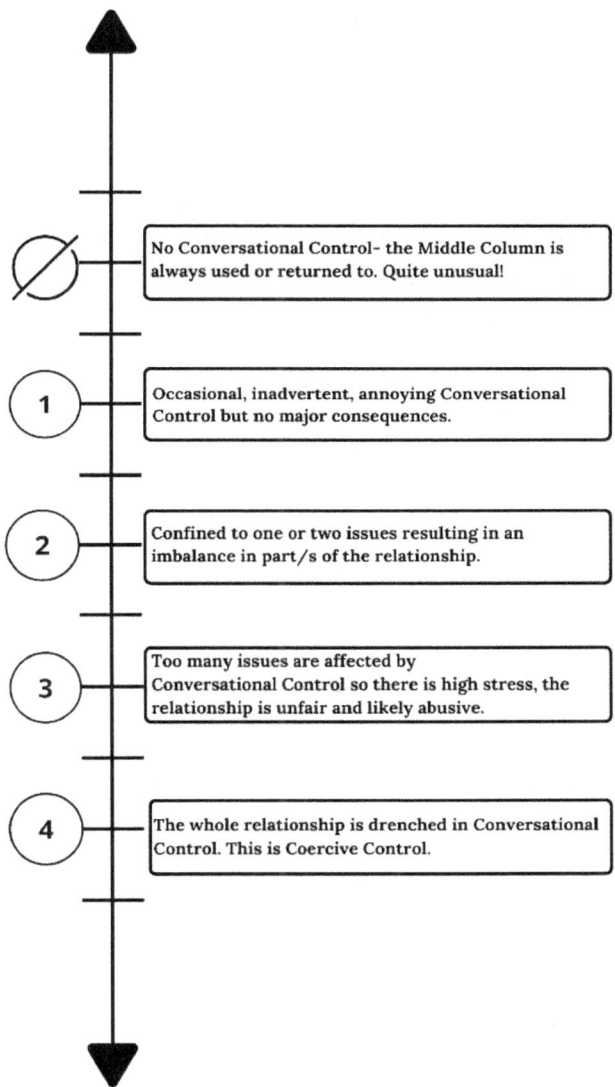

Diagram 3 - The Levels of Conversational Control

Levels of Conversational Control

In my counselling room, I often see the effects on people who have relationships where there are Levels 1 - 4 of Conversational Control.

Level 1 is where there are occasional, irritating ways of talking 'at you' but not 'with you' or turning away from a conversation sometimes. For example, certain Arcing Up and Down tactics are common but it does not affect your rights or the equality of the relationship so much as it is temporarily annoying and upsetting. Long-standing issues are possible if not dealt with. The relationship is Relationally Just.

Level 2 is where some issues in the relationship are mismanaged because of Conversational Control but other areas of the relationship still function reasonably well. This is common for Level 1 and 2 relationships. For example, you may not use the Middle Column well when talking about finances, so you have arguments about money rather than agreements. This results in a more long-standing issues with negative consequences, such as feeling a lack of financial partnership and rights. Yet, other areas are easier to discuss. Overall, the relationship is Relationally Just.

Level 3, though, is where the Middle Column is not used enough for various important issues, leaving a sense of disconnection, stress, and emotional reactions. The higher-level use of Conversational Control creates more frequent arguments, and long-standing, unresolved issues. A greater percentage of these relationships fail because of Conversational Control. At this level, the relationship can be abusive. It is possible you will need help. The relationship certainly needs help. It is no longer equal or Relationally Just, as the degree of Conversational Control is too high. Too many issues are 'undiscussables' and much or most of the relationship is affected. If we really investigated the relationship, there would be a high degree of control and abuse.

Level 4 is when the entire relationship is drenched in Conversational Control. One partner systematically takes over their partner's life and prevents them from having an equal say in any aspect of the relationship.

This is serious, dangerous, and is the level of Coercive Control. The overall consequence is that you are no longer in charge of your life because the level of Conversational Control is so high.

It means you can't have equal or any input into how the relationship is run, or any autonomy to direct your own life. There is no Middle Column possible. Level 4 means you need help. The relationship is not safe.

People who use Conversational Control may not consciously know, understand, identify or be able to define what they are doing. They just know it works to get their own way. This can be because of poor role modelling or lack of care, or it can be intentional and a desire to control.

At the heart of it all are patterns that will harm any relationship, such as:

- not asking each other good questions to understand each other's needs and perspective,
- avoiding, refusing, mishandling, or shutting down topics that need to be discussed,
- or forcing discussions around topics that don't need to be discussed.

These things happen when not enough time is spent where we can discuss things without fear, fix things, and apologise when needed. What's great about the Middle Column is that we feel safe because there is goodwill; we feel respected, cared for, and shown interest by the other person. And that matters a lot when we need to talk, right?

Conversational Rights

We have the right to be treated respectfully in all conversations. Imagine if we were taught that from a young age. It would make such a difference! We have as much right in a conversation to be heard and have our point of view taken into consideration as the other person does. This may sound simple, but it may not have been role-modelled to us; in fact, it is not usually even talked about as a thing we need to consider.

Conversations are often just 'had' without any skills or real thought, and certainly no reflection. Think of how we have been spoken to or bullied by our parents, teachers, colleagues, or bosses. What we observe growing up and in our everyday life impacts us. For example, what we see and hear in the media, in our social settings, with peers, and even in the political arena.

If we take this a bit further, the idea of Conversational Rights means that in any conversation, we have the right to feel psychologically and emotionally safe, and there is a sense of goodwill, respect, empathy, patience, reciprocity, and collaboration.

No matter how clever we are or how hard we try, we can rarely process a slow, let alone a fast-paced, set of Unfair Conversational Tactics.

To do so takes knowledge, skills, practice, and confidence, and many of us don't have these or are unaware of our Conversational Rights. This is why I have developed the framework I am teaching you in this book, because once we can look at conversations through the lens of Conversational Control, we can identify, process, and respond to Unfair Conversational Tactics with the skill and confidence to protect ourselves and to make the changes that are right for us in our relationships.

It is so familiar to hear things like, 'You just need to set boundaries,' or 'Just say this in response,' or 'I would never put up with that,' when you talk with someone to try to make sense of what is happening. It can feel like we should know how to handle specific conversations. However, not many people can understand, let alone process, Conversational Control when it is happening. They know it feels wrong. The funny thing is that even having to process Conversational Control is unfair.

When the Middle Column is avoided and Unfair Conversational Tactics are used, it cannot be defined as a conversation. It is more of a power struggle, someone trying to 'win' the conversation than actually having it...and wasting time and energy. If we attempt to process it, we can go around in circles.

So, having a framework and knowledge to work from helps us understand what happens in the conversations in our relationships and, most importantly, what we can do about it. We can develop the skills and confidence needed to ensure that conversations in our relationships are healthier or that we only have people with healthier conversational styles in our lives!

Conversational Equality

We can stand firm on the idea that we have Conversational Rights no matter how the other person speaks with us. We also need Conversational Equality for any relationship to feel good. This is only present when people acknowledge and *believe* in your Conversational Rights!

Essentially, Conversational Equality means that you not only have Conversational Rights, but they are respected. You know your psychological and emotional safety is respected, and you *have* a sense of goodwill, respect, empathy, patience, reciprocity, and collaboration from the other person rather than just the *right* to those things. In such a relationship, we know we can sort things out, even clumsily and over time, because both people want its benefits and the lovely sense of connection it creates.

It is wonderful, isn't it, being around people who have goodwill towards us and want to make us feel safe with them? It is a different energy that some of us have only felt with certain people in our lives.

Emotional Consequences

It is common for my clients to express how they don't feel heard, seen, or respected in one or more areas or the whole relationship. This can lead to depression, anxiety, loneliness, and disconnection. These are just some of the emotional consequences.

Some clients become deeply sad or angry about the conversations over specific issues as in Level 2, such as being unable to talk about their fears, extended family issues, money, or unfair differences in who does the housework/shopping/cooking/cleaning. There is a pattern of conversational difficulty over an issue.

As we progress to Level 3 and 4 of Conversational Control, the emotional consequences are dire. Many of my clients have felt suicidal, or like they were more like a cardboard cut-out than real; they felt trapped, shamed, and fearful of retaliation.

The Wedge – An Overall Effect

The unresolved consequences of Conversational Control will drive a wedge between people, particularly intimate partners. An example from my counselling room is when a person or partner faults my client's personality, beliefs, talents, and ideas instead of staying in the Middle Column and addressing the issue my client is trying to discuss. It becomes traumatising, and the wedge is very deep.

The wedge between Sarah and Mark keeps being hammered deeper because Mark uses constant Conversational Control. Until he becomes aware of it, and they can both have conversations that work, the wedge will keep being driven deeper. Even worse for my clients, like Sarah, is when someone does not have the awareness, skills, or goodwill to acknowledge their impact and make amends. In couples counselling, this is such a common problem.

Questions We Can Consider About Our Conversations

I always ask people in a relationship about what conversations worry them. I check whether they find the conversations around specific issues more:

- Adversarial or empathic
- Confusing or clear
- Combative or collaborative
- Retaliatory or reconciliating

The answers to the above help us map out how the communication happens in the relationship, and around what issues or in which situations the conversations tend to become tricky.

Be Wary of Diagnosing

Bill and Bob enjoyed their relationship. There was no obvious power imbalance; both wanted a healthy relationship. However, Bill would not talk with Bob well regarding certain issues in the relationship. For Bill, it was difficult to discuss household roles. He was not that interested, and without realising it, he shut down many of Bob's attempts to discuss how they divided the chores between them.

Bill routinely Arced Up by getting sarcastic and defensive, or Arced Down by being bored and evasive. Bob wondered why this was. Was it the way he was raising it? Was it Bill's upbringing, family of origin issues, his culture, or some sort of trauma? Bob found himself irritated and hurt. He felt blocked and didn't want to upset Bill or cause a rupture in their relationship. He loved Bill. He knew Bill loved him. But eventually, Bob's hurt and frustration infiltrated other areas of the relationship. He lost some attraction to Bill and was less inclined to take up the slack that Bill's lack of effort was leaving. Bill continued to shun the issue, and the relationship turned a corner.

What was happening to Bob was unfair. He found himself running the household and avoiding making Bill angry or sulky. This 'undiscussable' created havoc. It was time for Bob to understand how Bill avoided the Middle Column.

Neither Bill or Bob are toxic, narcissistic, or abusive. They had no idea how the lack and type of conversations would tilt their relationship off course. They also didn't understand how the tension between them affected their extended family, including the younger, watchful generation and beloved friends. Even the dog felt the tension at times.

Often, the Unfair Conversational Tactics used are very subtle, petty even, and it is good for us to remember that their use does not indicate that the person using them is unpleasant, abusive or has a personality problem such as Narcissistic Personality Disorder. I don't think it is helpful to categorise people as 'a narcissist', for example, or to aim for perfect, sanitised conversations. It is human and commonplace to use some tactics of Conversational Control occasionally.

Bill needed education, not a diagnosis. Once it was explained to him, he got it. He felt ridiculous about how he had impacted Bob. He made amends. They sorted out other stuck places in their relationship.

It's helpful to aim to become aware of when we are using or experiencing Conversational Control and to note the consequences. The trouble begins if we are unaware or uncaring. It makes matters worse to blame someone for a problem that could have been resolved if the Middle Column had been used, but we were unaware or refused to do so.

When we Justify, Argue, Defend or Explain ourselves in response to an Unfair Conversational Tactic, it is usually because we are seeking the Middle Column where we can regain some goodwill in the form of some:

- Agreement
- Permission
- Understanding
- Reassurance
- Connection

Let's look back at Sarah and Mark. Sarah would try to get goodwill from Mark when he accused her of overspending. She was essentially trying to get into the Middle Column. They weren't grasping the bigger picture, that Mark was being disrespectful, secretive, and controlling around money because he earned it and was denying Sarah equal say in how their money was spent. He frequently started fights about money.

Sarah would respond by either:

Justifying: 'But I spent that money on our children, not on me.'

Defending: 'I am not overspending; I hardly spent anything last week and the kids and I went without.'

Explaining: 'Well, the kids needed sports registration fees and ballet shoes.'

Arguing: 'How come you're so worried about what I spend? What are *you* spending?'

Now, sometimes these responses can work depending on the type of Conversational Control we are up against. However, often, they have no effect. Your response will only be considered if the person realises they are ruining the conversation, they need to get into a fair mindset, and they must be more respectful to make it possible.

No matter how hard someone like Sarah tries, the Marks of the world will more often than not respond using another Arcing Up or Arcing Down tactic. He withholds good will, avoids the Middle Column, and the cycle continues. Sarah will inevitably feel an even more profound sense of anxiety, fear, obligation, guilt, shame, or confusion, whether the same or a different blend than before.

Then, Sarah might seek to connect with Mark or get his agreement, permission, understanding, or reassurance in the same or a different way than she had tried before. Around it goes. If the Middle Column is not used, we tend to submit, cater, or give up eventually.

When these conversations are too regular or happen in too many areas of the relationship, the relationship is in danger of tipping into unhealthy zones and becoming unfair.

This is a typical cycle of Conversational Control:

1. Mark accuses Sarah.
2. Sarah justifies, argues, defends, or explains herself.
3. Mark withholds the agreement, permission, understanding, reassurance, or connection Sarah is seeking.
4. Mark uses another tactic to keep her trying.
5. He will not give her what she is seeking.
6. Mark is refusing the Middle Column and controls the conversation.
7. Sarah is left high and dry and gives up.

Self-Awareness

Knowing where we get caught up and how we might use Conversational Control ourselves is also helpful. It's easy to get caught up in how everyone communicates with us without also considering how we communicate, where we easily stay in the Middle Column and where we might use Unfair Conversational Tactics.

When we enter any relationship, we could all pay more attention to how the other person handles conversations and manages misunderstandings. It is astute to ask ourselves, can this person have conversations that work, or are conversations likely to become a power struggle over specific issues? Unfortunately, some people will not understand or accept the notion of Conversational Rights or Conversational Equality, and the relationship will skew towards their conversational limitations and their pattern of Arcing Up and Arcing Down. And yes, we must ask ourselves the same question about our ability to stay in or return to the Middle Column.

We are all so different in how we are affected by Conversational Control. It is good to notice this about ourselves. It's common for someone to apologise for your feelings rather than how they treated you. This is an apology without any substance or meaning. For example, it is not helpful to hear, 'I'm sorry you feel that way,' or 'I'm sorry you felt dismissed,' as what has been left out is the tactic that was used to bring that about. It is far more helpful to hear, 'I'm sorry for how I mishandled the conversation/treated you/dismissed you, brushed off your feelings/criticised you,' as that is an apology with substance. They have acknowledged the aspects of their behaviour that have impacted you. There is the possibility of repair.

Funnily enough, all my longer-term relationships are always in the Middle Column, so as a result, I have developed a deep sense of emotional and psychological safety. We have goodwill. It feels safe and nice. Apologies are generous if and when they are ever necessary.

I have also taken note of my tendencies to use Conversational Control. Even though I love being in or returning to the Middle Column, as I look back over my life, I see that there have been many times I have failed to do this, and I have missed the point or hurt others. The important thing for me is to repair and apologise.

5

How to Respond to Conversational Control

As I grew up, I had no idea of my rights, conversational or otherwise. It was easy for parents, teachers, or anyone to get me to cater or submit because I couldn't emotionally manage their disapproval or their disappointment whether it was a look, a comment or behaviour. Of course, I still struggle with this! We are all prone to it to some extent, often out of our awareness and from a deep, unconscious level. That is, unless we have psychopathic tendencies.

These diagrams sum up how many of us naturally react to Conversational Control, because we can't identify the tactics used or how they control us, and so we give in.

Diagram 4 - Conversational Control

Diagram 5 - How We Respond

In a relationship, if we experience a strong pattern of Unfair Conversational Tactics, if it is heading towards the higher Levels of 3, where many issues are 'undiscussable', or Level 4, where no issues are discussable, we are being gradually trained to behave in a compliant manner. This can be in many issues and areas of the relationship, or the entire relationship.

The word 'groomed' suggests being trained, primed, and prepared for something; that's what someone using a Level 3 or 4 pattern of Conversational Control is doing in many ways. They are priming you, unconsciously or strategically, to follow their idea of conversations and what they are able or willing to address and what they aren't. The relationship becomes an arrangement that suits the other person better. Unfortunately, the more we unconsciously avoid disappointing or distressing the other person, even at our expense, the more we feel unable to raise issues, discuss topics, or make changes. Then we are more likely to be 'trainable' or 'groomable' in at least some areas of the relationship.

Take Mark, for example. He has gradually trained Sarah to give in to his Arcing Up and Arcing Down when she tries to raise issues around sex or money. The effect on Sarah is that her life revolves around Mark; her life is restrained by the budget Mark has put her on, she is unable to provide extras for the children, and the domination, lack of discussion and connection are putting her off sex.

How to Detect Patterns in Conversational Control - Zooming In and Zooming Out

If we focus on how each conversation goes and what sort of Unfair Tactics are used, we miss the pattern at play and the relationship's big picture. We cannot afford to constantly zoom in like that. It is too simplistic. Instead, we must zoom out and look at the overall relationship. Someone like Mark will use zooming-in tactics and keep their attention on a very limited part of the conversation, away from the bigger picture of the relationship. He will use Unfair

Conversational Tactics to control the conversation towards what's wrong with Sarah rather than the fact he is not creating a relationship but training Sarah into accepting an arrangement that only suits him.

If Mark zoomed out and looked at his effect on Sarah, he would notice he was compromising and restricting Sarah, as well as the children. He was not allowing Sarah equality. If he were not an abusive person, he would make the changes and maybe seek help. He is not a viable partner if he can't or won't accept that he has no right to control a person or a relationship. This is the same for any gender.

When we are willing and able to switch between zooming in and out, we can also see a clear difference between someone Arcing Up or Down in response to being treated poorly and with disrespect, and someone Arcing Up or Down to control the conversation. Somebody zooming in will accuse us of Arcing Up or Arcing Down in response to their disrespectful comments. 'Don't raise your voice at me,' or 'You always carry on like this,' as that accusation deflects attention away from their initial disrespect.

Zooming out makes the pattern clear in a conversation as well as over the entire relationship. We often fail to zoom out and instead focus on small parts of a relationship or certain conversations rather than how it is all connected into a pattern.

Questions to Ask Ourselves About Our Tolerance Levels

We all have different tolerance levels to Arcing Up and Down, so when someone sends out signals of disappointment, distress, disapproval, or disgust, there will be a certain point at which we cater or submit to those signals and go into an unconscious reaction pattern or a trauma response.

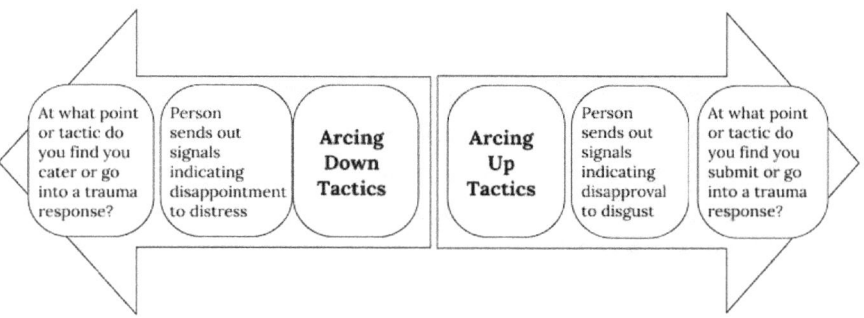

Diagram 6 - Our Tipping Point

It's wise to ask ourselves:

- What level of disappointment can we tolerate?
- What level of distress brings us undone?
- What level of disapproval really gets to us?
- What happens to us if we see disgust on their face, hear it in their tone, or see it in their body language?
- When we react to their control, what are we seeking? Connection, agreement, approval, reassurance, or permission?
- What headspace do we go into? For example, do we go into some level of confusion, fear, anxiety, obligation, guilt, confusion, depression, or shame?

It's fascinating and revealing to reflect on our tolerance for Unfair Conversational Tactics, where we can stay calmly aware of our rights and needs. At what point, or with which tactic, does it 'get' to us, and cause us to cater or defer without thinking?

When I think about my own level of tolerance, I am particularly affected by a dismissive and condescending attitude, body language, vocal tone, and words by someone I thought I was either developing or had a connection with. It has always silenced me into shock and confusion. If there isn't a recognition of the impact and an apology with substance, the relationship is less likely to be repairable, and I lose interest.

The Response Framework - Identify then Respond

Identifying Conversational Control and learning how to respond are skills. We've all heard responding is better than reacting, but developing these skills can take time. Some relationships will have more hope than others that changes can be made. However, we will at least feel calmer and more able to recognise and resist where we are habitually or unconsciously catering or submitting.

We can also become more aware of what it costs us to defer, where we have to avoid some conversations, or where we have our efforts shut down. There is no wisdom in someone controlling any conversation, particularly when it's a pattern that reduces the quality of a relationship. Yet it is how humans have evolved.

Many people dare not raise certain issues because there are so many Arcing Up or Down tactics to deal with, so they instinctively avoid them. Sally, for example, didn't raise with her partner, Josh, how she felt about their sexual relationship and his desire to use sex toys without any warmth or connection. Over time, she had come to detest this but couldn't find the courage to discuss it, because she knew from experience that her partner won't hear her and have a balanced conversation. It was more likely he would Arc Up in various ways to make her feel guilty and, therefore, submit to him. What if Josh had gotten into the Middle Column and asked her what she wanted and how they could improve things between them?

The Response Framework helps guide us in a conversation that has left the Middle Column for dust! It can be so easy to lose our bearings when the conversation has become a power struggle, so having a framework can make it easier to work out what to say and do.

Imagine having several choices when faced with somebody talking 'at' or down to us, as in Arcing Up, or turning away from us, as in Arcing Down. As they are not talking with us in a way that intends collaboration or connection, it's really helpful if we know how to respond without needlessly seeking their agreement, permission, reassurance, or understanding by justifying, arguing, defending, or explaining ourselves. Trying to explain ourselves to someone not in the Middle Column and not listening with intent to understand is frustrating. I have given my power away countless times, trying to justify myself to someone who has absolutely no intention of responding from the Middle Column and trying to understand my perspective. They simply switch to another tactic in response to my efforts. It feels so defeating, and a pattern of this is a sure way for any relationship to falter.

Many people worry about using Conversational Control themselves when they respond using the Response Framework. These techniques aren't for manipulating or controlling your partner. Quite the opposite. They intend to shift the relationship back to a more equal playing field. At the very least, they help us clear things up within ourselves, even if shifting the conversation isn't possible. For example, we can see what they are doing with the conversation, and we know it is not about us but about the way they are communicating. We are also positioned to consider whether we are dealing with a person who cares how we feel and is open to the Middle Column or not.

It's essential to always use the techniques in a way that feels right for you, changing some words or the whole phrase to suit how you usually speak. You'll gain confidence quicker if you feel the words are more authentic.

The basis of the Response Framework is to shift the conversation back into the Middle Column. That's how we know we are not using Conversational Control ourselves: because we respond in a way that invites and guides the conversation and the relationship back to an equal playing field.

I have a very annoying habit of becoming so involved in observing any tactics of Conversational Control that are being used against me that I can completely forget to respond. So, I am left with the fact that I didn't use any of the Response Framework even to try to move the conversation towards the Middle Column. This has cost me because I did not stand up for myself, and they got away with controlling the conversation.

A Clean Response

Before I outline the four possibilities and what to avoid, I want to discuss what I mean by a 'clean response'. To respond cleanly, you would stay as non-reactive as possible. It is helpful to use short, simple, phrases, and powerful to use invitational suggestions, as in the following examples:

- **How about we**…speak respectfully.
- **Let's**…discuss this peaceably.
- **Let's not**…use blame and shame.
- **I suggest**…we hear each other out.
- **Why don't we**…work towards a win/win
- **What say we**…try again?
- **Can we**…listen to each other's perspective?
- **What would it take**…to work towards a compromise?

We are not pointing the finger and telling someone what we think about them at that moment or what they are doing wrong (even if we strongly feel that they are in the wrong). Nor are we catering or submitting. We suggest what could be done instead. See the difference? It's a masterstroke as we leave no room for even the most ardent users of Conversational Control to get too far with us. Clean responses are more powerful than responding emotionally. However, under duress, it can be so hard to use clean responses when you are being Conversationally Controlled.

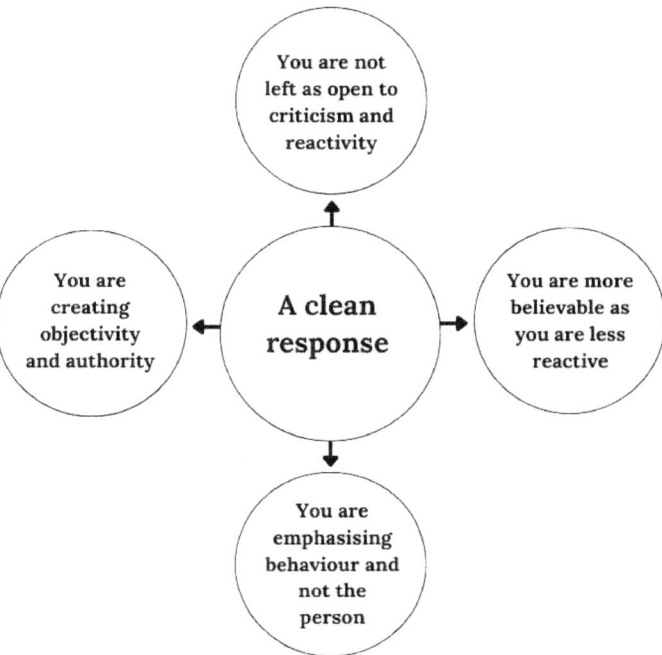

Diagram 7 - A Clean Response

It can feel unfair to say, 'I suggest *we* hear each other out,' when we are the one being talked at, over the top of, or interrupted, and we feel annoyed. We have to give up the idea of 'hitting back'.

Using clean and non-blaming phrases that ask their current behaviour to stop and state what would be healthier and more respectful for both of you is hard for even the most ardent controller of conversations to ignore. It's also difficult for someone to use an Unfair Conversational Tactic in response to our invitational phrases without looking quite foolish.

Remembering short and simple phrases is much easier when we feel stressed.

When we use these phrases, we are not controlling the conversation. We are directing the conversation to a healthier possibility. This takes our power back.

Many Unfair Conversational Tactics don't affect me very much now, unless it is in a group situation. Then it becomes very complex and requires an uninvested person to keep the conversation clean and on track. One-on-one, I can usually stay as grounded as possible to consider how I respond. This means observing myself, remembering to breathe, focusing on what is around me and taking time to respond. Most importantly, it gives me strength just remembering that I have Conversational Rights, and that aiming for Conversational Equality is healthy for all concerned. Then, I am in a good position to use the Response Framework.

Is the Other Person Willing or Able?

I can't stress enough that when we start responding cleanly, and the person we're talking with won't shake themselves out of Conversational Control, it soon becomes clear whether they are willing or able to meet us in the Middle Column.

We become more aware of the tactics used to control the conversation because we see what is happening. Now, we have a better chance of finding ways to respond and shift the conversation to the more productive and safer zone (the Middle Column) rather than get stuck in a useless reaction cycle and possibly become traumatised. I say 'a better chance' because it can take some time to stop reacting to attitudes, behaviours and tactics that are our sore spots.

Can you see how we have more solid ground when we know we aim for the Middle Column? Still, the other person could be unable or unwilling to and prefers the 'blame, define and defame game'. This is where we are told how and why we are the problem and put down for it.

One of my elderly clients was very controlled by her partner to the point that he made her come home early from an overseas trip. She said to me, with tears in her eyes, 'He says I am just selfish and self-pitying. Do you think I am? He told our friends how selfish I am.'

Such comments blamed her, defined her personality, and then defamed her to others, which worked well to shame her. These comments also drew attention away from how selfish and self-pitying *he* had been to coerce her to cut her overseas trip short to look after him, despite the fact she had waited for a long time for this trip, which had been very important to her. He never thanked her for this. She was so Conversationally Controlled that she could not zoom out and see the bigger picture.

This is a normal effect of a pattern of control. We stop being able to evaluate the relationship critically and what is happening, and we zoom in to what was said instead because we are just trying to cope in that moment.

My heart goes out to those people in my counselling room who have said to me over the years, 'But he/she/they said I was just stubborn/fat/mean/slow/mentally ill/neurotic/ or demented.' They were trying to determine if they were and what they should do about it. They didn't understand that these were Arcing Up tactics designed to throw them off course, focus back on themselves, and do what their conversational partner wanted. Remember, as soon as we feel anything approaching anxiety, fear, obligation, guilt, shame, or confusion, we are off-kilter and very easy to control conversationally. My elderly client had been well trained to feel shame, and therefore cater or submit to her partner.

Remember, it's highly stressful when someone starts using Unfair Conversational Tactics towards us. We can become ungrounded, rattled, and unable to think well. It's a normal response that so many of us kick ourselves for afterwards. We think, 'Why didn't I just say…' But when we're up against someone who is attempting to blame, define or defame us, our nervous systems pick up the threat, and we might go into the Response Cycle or go straight into a defensive, argumentative, anxious or shocked trauma response.

At the very least, when we understand what's happening when faced with blaming tactics such as, 'you're so insecure' or 'you're such a nag', it's easier to recognise the Conversational Control and not take it on. When we avoid the trap of wondering if they are right, it is easier to stay in our boots, recognise the tactic, consider our response, and insist on a shift in the conversation towards the Middle Column. Even if we feel anxious on the inside, our outside self must appear self-contained, or at least non-reactive.

This is not easy. For some of us, staying 'calm' feels totally unfair when we are being treated disrespectfully. We don't give our power away, though, if our face and body are reasonably composed and we act like we are not being 'led' by their tactics.

Over time, if we zoom out, we can decide if it was a one-off incident or a pattern of Conversational Control, and whether the relationship will be in the Middle Column enough for our liking. People who are using Conversational Control must learn or be made aware that they are communicating unfairly and either lack the skills or interest to reach the Middle Column. Some will respond to us well, and some simply can't. They don't have the capacity in a particular situation for whatever reason. Or maybe they don't have the capacity in general, but more to the point, they don't wish to learn. This makes them less safe to discuss things with and more likely to be hurtful and combative. Some people are just not interested in communicating well! Any relationship with them will end up with their partner experiencing a level of Conversational Control where growth or emotional intimacy is impossible.

To show you the Response Framework, I have inserted it into the Conversational Control Framework so you have a visual memory you can use when under pressure.

There are four ways to respond to Conversational Control cleanly: you can Counter the tactic, Redirect the person back towards the Middle Column, Call out the tactic, and Exit the conversation if it is not working. Using these pushbacks enables us to refuse the invitation to give away our power. We must Avoid catering, submitting or going into the reaction cycle or a trauma response.

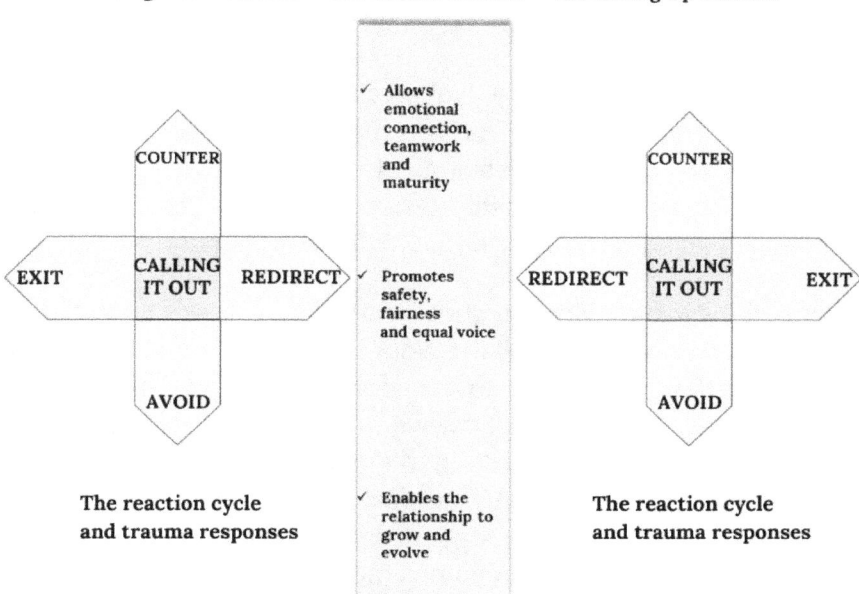

Diagram 8 - Response Framework

Countering

This is a healthy, clean pushback. We must know the main strategies central to Conversational Control to counter well. These are Unfair Conversational Tactics that:

1. Use questions that are demanding, wheedling, argumentative, or destabilising
2. Use deflection
3. Imply urgency for you to respond
4. Interrupt you
5. Define, blame, and defame you

Let's focus on how to respond to someone using questions to keep control of the conversation. Questions framed as a win/lose are usually detrimental and aimed at showing us how wrong we are. For example, 'Why do you always have to be so analytical?' Any way we answer this will put us in the wrong. Questions are a commonly unrecognised tactic of Conversational Control.

When facing this tactic, we first evaluate the intent behind the question. Win/lose questions are not about reaching mutual understanding but are designed to provoke your emotional response. They make you justify, argue, defend, or explain yourself, ultimately leading us to cater or submit to their demands.

Look at the cycle of win/lose questions below and see how it gives away our power as we do all the work to keep the conversation fair and respectful. It's normal to respond like this when we try to connect and sort things out. However, the other person might want different things and have no intention of heading to the Middle Column, so it is unfair. Here, one person who is upset about their date changing their arrangements uses an unfair list of questions to control the conversation. It becomes more like an interrogation than trying to understand what happened.

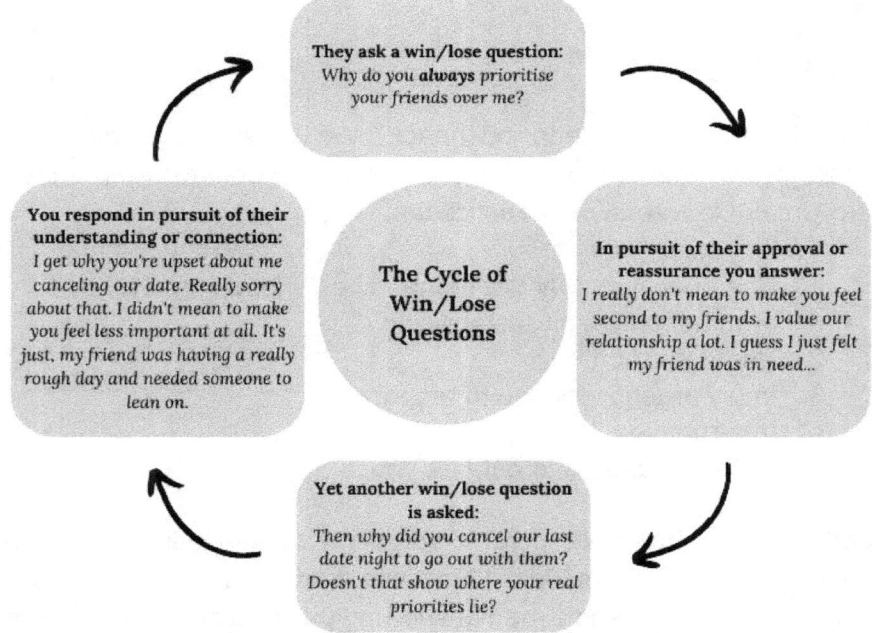

Diagram 9 - Cycle of Win/Lose Questions

Why Am I Answering This – Checking the Intent of the Question

On one level, continuing to question someone like in the diagrams is unremarkable and extremely common. Yet, asking win/lose questions, where there is an assumption that you are in the wrong and have to explain yourself, is unfair.

Firstly, it always pays to ask ourselves, 'Why am I answering this?' and 'Should I be answering this?' Use one of the 'softening' phrases below to check out their intent:

- I am curious…how is this useful/helpful?
- I am wondering…what are you aiming for here?
- Can you tell me…where is this line of questioning going?
- I am not clear…why does this matter?
- What would you say…is the point of this discussion?
- I'd like to understand…why are you asking me this?

By using these phrases, we are working towards the Middle Column and avoiding the combativeness of their questioning. The guideline is to answer a question or a set of questions that seem intrusive and unfair with an open question like the above. It is a clean way of responding.

It also prevents us from being drawn into a never-ending cycle of answering their questions. No matter what we say, our answer will be rebuffed, disputed, mocked, or ridiculed, and we will face another question. We are well and truly on the back foot. Nothing is gained by answering somebody who is not using the Middle Column. Yet, we are all prone to falling for this tactic.

Deflections

Deflections occur when someone wants to avoid discussing a particular topic.

For example, changing the subject or turning the discussion on to something you have done or said that they didn't like.

Jack: 'I find it hard when you mock me in front of our friends.'

Jill: 'What about you when you tell me to watch my mouth in front of the children!'

This is a way to stay 'on top' and control the conversation. Some people don't realise they are deflecting and will willingly stop when we ask them. Others will object to us refusing to be taken off track and will continue to try to dominate or control the conversation in another way. To stop deflections, here are some suggestions:

- We are not talking about that…we are talking about this…
- That may be…but we are talking about…
- How about…we sort this issue first.
- Let's stay on track.
- I suggest we…stay focused.
- Why don't we…stick to one topic at a time.
- What say we…finish this first.

If we respond by switching to the topic that they switch to, it is the same as answering questions that are to keep you deferring to them; the conversation goes around in circles, and nothing gets resolved. It also leaves us hurt, unheard and disconnected. To feel safer and more independent of tactics, it is critical to recognise deflections and use a clean response.

Urgency

A sense of urgency or other forms of duress can be used to pressure us into agreeing or responding to something. For example, 'I really need to know right this minute if you will loan me the money to pay off my bill, or else I am in strife.' When someone uses urgency to make us feel like we have to decide, agree, do, or answer something right now 'or else' – use healthy delaying techniques:

- Let's not decide in a hurry.
- How about we discuss this?
- I suggest we think this over.
- I need to think about that.
- I will consider it.
- I will get back to you with my thoughts.
- We must consider this carefully.

Interruptions

Interruptions are often combined with unfair questions, deflections, and a sense of urgency that derails us when we valiantly try to justify, argue, or defend ourselves and seek something from the Middle Column. Interruptions used as a Conversational Control tactic are more than simply cutting you off; they are used with the intention to take over and win the conversation.

Here are some helpful, clean phrases:

- One minute…
- Let me finish.
- Let's listen to each other.
- I suggest we hear each other out.
- Let's not interrupt one another.
- How about we let each other finish.
- Depending on the circumstance, you can be silent during the interruption, then, without missing a beat or responding to their interruptions, pick up where you left off and say: 'What I was in the process of saying was…'

With all this said, please note that, like all tactics, someone may question, deflect, interrupt or use urgency just because they are excited or stressed, but they are not trying to control us. The key is knowing the difference between whether they are trying to win the conversation rather than having it.

Differences of Opinion

When somebody is hellbent on controlling the conversation, they fail to see or respect the fact that we may have a different opinion, viewpoint, or perspective to them. It is critical and only fair that our perspective is addressed, asked about and acknowledged. When this doesn't happen, it is a wrecking ball for any relationship. The failure to seek the other person's ideas, thoughts or opinions, and ask good questions to elicit these, is one of the main problems I see between couples and people in general.

This is not a well-taught skill; many people don't know how to ask helpful questions, and it limits the level of connection and growth possible in any relationship. Getting to know the other person requires good-hearted questions. So, if this is or has been a problem in your relationships, you know the pain of somebody unwilling or unable to do that. Depending on the level of Conversational Control and the person's ability, interest, or motivation to have conversations that work, these are skills that can be learnt.

First, use a countering option, then you can follow up with an invitation to the Middle Column where questions and sharing perspectives can happen without trying to override one another. Here are some counters:

- That may be, but I see it differently.
- It's okay that we have different opinions, but let's talk about it respectfully.
- We see it differently.
- That's your opinion.
- I have a different opinion to you.
- That is your perspective.
- We have two different views here.
- I understand, but my view is…
- I see your point, and I see it differently.
- My opinion is still valid.

Redirecting

Redirecting is where we invite the other person back towards the Middle Column. There are clean and straightforward ways that you can redirect, and it can work so well. Knowing that we have the right to suggest a move back into the Middle Column, and that it is the only way to resolve something, can provide some harbour in a storm. I personally rely on this type of response more easily than the others.

The main thing to note about redirecting is that we are backing off from being adversarial. We are not trying to solve the problem, most likely because we can tell it won't happen. However, we retain our power by not running away. Rather, we're respectfully taking the lead, showing that we'd like the conversation to remain or return to the Middle Column. You can use redirecting phrases such as:

- How about we speak nicely to each other?
- How about we listen to each other?
- What say we listen to each other's perspectives?
- I suggest we ask each other some helpful questions.
- Let's discuss this fairly/reasonably.
- Let's avoid blaming each other.
- Let's keep our voices down.
- Let's talk about something else for a bit; this doesn't seem to be going anywhere.
- I suggest we use a kinder tone.
- Can we be on the same team?
- Can we respect each other's opinions?
- Why don't we change direction?
- What about we each have a say?
- What say we start this conversation again?
- What say we consider each other's needs here?

I often pair a countering response with redirecting. It is a clean, assertive, yet non-confrontational blend of responses.

- **Counter:** What are you aiming for here? **Then Redirect:** What about we each have a say?
- **Counter:** How is this useful? **Then Redirect:** Why don't we change direction?
- **Counter:** Where is this line of questioning going? **Then Redirect:** Let's avoid blaming each other.
- **Counter:** Why does this matter? **Then Redirect:** What say we consider each other's needs here?
- **Counter:** I see it differently. **Then Redirect:** Why don't we ask each other about our different perspectives?

Calling It Out

Calling it out can be the most challenging way of responding to Conversational Control. This is because it is more confrontational. We are actively pointing out their behaviour. Therefore, we must be prepared for a possible upsurge in Arcing Up or Down.

For this reason, it isn't a technique I use often. I'm also not usually able to think fast enough to call it out. It seems much easier for me to counter and even easier for me to redirect. We are all different and will have preferred ways of responding healthily.

However, there may be a moment when we feel comfortable or where it feels particularly appropriate. It works a treat for somebody who has become heated and is unaware of what they are doing.

If you call it out, remember to be as non-reactive as possible and try to use a normal tone. It is not about being argumentative. We are still trying to return to the Middle Column respectfully, and calling it out may be necessary to get there. Pairing calling it out with redirecting is a clean and powerful combination of responses that leaves them in no uncertainty that we are not playing their game—we are playing a healthier game.

Here are some subtle ways to call it out:

- Are you aware you are using X tactic right now?
- This conversation doesn't feel safe.
- This conversation doesn't feel fair.
- This conversation isn't productive.
- Do you realise you're taking over this conversation?
- Do you realise you haven't been listening to me?
- Do you think the way you're speaking to me is respectful/appropriate?
- Would you be okay with me asking you that type of question?

These are more direct ways of calling it out:

- I would appreciate it if you stopped pushing me to give in.
- It is not acceptable for you to speak to me like that.
- It's time for you to stop arcing up/arcing down/getting aggressive/playing the victim.
- That type of comment is inappropriate.
- That type of question is unfair.
- You keep interrupting me/mocking me—I will not accept this behaviour.
- At what point will you realise you can't speak to me like that?
- That's enough.
- That's unacceptable.
- Stop.

Exit

Exiting the conversation is often the best course of action when countering, redirecting, calling it out, or a combination of these doesn't move the conversation back to the Middle Column. In other words, it's time to end the conversation when you can tell they won't be backing down, and you will be wasting your breath to continue trying. It can be done in a way that doesn't single them out as being 'in the wrong'. Or it could be more pointed. For example, suppose the other person is being very inappropriate. In that case, you can call it out before exiting.

You can also see that it can be coupled with redirecting. This is a powerful combination that, again, can be gentle or more pointed.

We can, of course, redirect and then point out that if the conversation can't change course, we will exit or take a break from the conversation until it is in the Middle Column. For example:

Redirect: How about we speak nicely to each other? **Then Exit:** Otherwise, I think we should end this for now.

Redirect: How about we listen to each other? **Then Exit:** Otherwise, I'm going to tap out.

Redirect: Let's discuss this reasonably. **Then Exit:** Otherwise, let's take a break.

Redirect: Let's avoid blaming each other. **Then Exit:** Otherwise, we need to end the conversation.

Redirect: I suggest we use a kinder tone. **Then Exit:** Or have this conversation another time.

Redirect: I think we should be more appropriate around the children. **Then Exit:** So, I will leave until that can happen.

Reactions and Responses to Avoid

We want to avoid the reactions and responses that give away our power. This means recognising when we are going into any level of anxiety, fear, obligation, guilt, shame or confusion and that those reactions can make it difficult for us to think. We also avoid seeking their reassurance, permission, agreement, or approval by justifying, arguing, defending or explaining ourselves. We will naturally start to do that in the face of Unfair

Conversational Tactics. It is normal to try and establish or get back some connection. The trouble is, we are doing that from the back foot and putting ourselves in the firing line for more Conversational Control. Once we become aware, we know to switch to one of the phrases outlined in the Response Framework instead.

We get better at this over time. It is impossible to keep up with the speed and skill with which some people use Unfair Conversational Tactics.

To keep our sanity, it is wise to avoid using 'I' or 'You' phrases. Even though it may make sense to do so at the time, the following phrases can so easily start off more Arcing Up or Down and we are at risk of getting lost in another circular conversation where we end up giving away our power. For example, avoid saying:

- You make me…
- You need to calm down…
- You are…
- You don't…
- You never…
- You always…
- I just think…
- If you loved me, you wouldn't…

Our goal is to avoid arguments, which allows for the Middle Column.

So, what do we say instead?

Great question!

- Instead of 'You need to calm down,' you could say, **'I can see why you are upset, however…'**
- Instead of 'You are being X,' you could say, **'Let's try and do Y instead.'**
- Instead of 'If you loved me, you would X,' you could say, **'Is this respectful?'**
- Instead of 'I feel X when you do that,' you could say, **'I see it this way…'**

Taking the emotional part out of responses and not blaming the other person encourages the conversation to be more respectful and helps us maintain ourselves.

One final point. Sometimes, it is safer or less energy consuming just to defer. There is no shame in that. The difference is that we know what we are doing and why we are doing it. We can see what we are up against. If we have to defer for our own safety, it is a sign we are being abused.

Moving Forward

So, now you have a framework from which to choose your responses. I think having one or two favourites of each type of response is helpful. Choose two favourite phrases you feel comfortable using when you decide to counter, redirect, call it out, or exit. It is more likely you will remember them when feeling stressed so that you open the possibility of shifting the conversation towards the Middle Column.

Remember that when we use these phrases, we create the possibility of goodwill, where combat is replaced by collaboration, and connection and growth are possible.

6

Higher Levels of Conversational Control – Coercive Control

I hope it is clear that even if a conversation appears harmless on the surface, if it is outside the Middle Column and stays there, it's unfair. It's as simple as that. At some stage, if a conversation gets adversarial, there has to be a return to the Middle Column if things are to work between people. And I'm sure you'll agree with me that it is so often the case that the Middle Column is never even thought about. So, over time, what might have been momentarily annoying becomes a pattern, creating a rift. Too many rifts erode the relationship to the point where it is less close, stable, or happy. The negative consequences can outweigh the benefits of the relationship.

At lower levels of Conversational Control, where Unfair Conversational Tactics tend to be confined to specific issues or areas of the relationship, there may be enough goodwill between people to fix this. It's about recognising and changing faulty communication by learning new skills. We all have to do that from time to time.

At higher levels of Conversational Control, the whole relationship is saturated in Unfair Conversational Tactics. One person repeatedly uses their own style and pattern of Arcing Up and Arcing Down tactics to groom the other, shaping them to suit their needs. Whether unconscious or strategic, one person is dictating what can and can't be talked about and will Arc Up or Arc Down at any attempt to move beyond what they 'permit'. The conversations are not equal, and neither is the relationship. It is more of an arrangement that benefits that particular person and is at the expense of the other.

From my studies, research and counselling, it seems likely that humans have thought it is okay to use someone like that since history has been recorded. It's challenging to comprehend how people using higher levels of Conversational Control can seem either pleased with, oblivious to, or unconcerned about their effect on others.

Attitudinal Style of Higher-Level Conversational Control

One critical factor leading to Conversational Control is a particular attitudinal style. Three components —**S**uperior, **E**ntitled and **A**dversarial—work together to create an attitude of domination, which can be very subtle and therefore tricky to detect. I refer to this attitudinal style as the SEA attitudinal style.

Superiority leads to a lack of concern with or empathy for the other person's feelings, perspective, and needs for emotional intimacy or equality within a relationship. Entitlement leads to expectations of one-way benefits and privileges. These mean communication will be adversarial to protect their superiority and their sense of entitlement to have their needs and wants met rather than yours. They will have a fault-finding, competitive style of communication that prevents self-reflection, compromise, change or growth.

The SEA attitudinal style is more momentary at the lower levels of Conversational Control; in other words, they do not always have a superior, entitled, and adversarial attitudinal style but rather occasionally behave as if they do. As we move along the continuum towards higher levels of Conversational Control, such as Level 3 and 4, this win/lose attitudinal style is more fixed. Some people *have*, rather than occasionally *use*, a superior, entitled, and adversarial attitude. Some people simply believe in their superiority over you and that they are entitled to take the lead. They will be adversarial, which means they will communicate in ways that are highly conversationally controlling.

It may well be the result of a poor upbringing, role modelling, or trauma. But a fixed superior, entitled, adversarial attitudinal style is not always about a rough past. Humans seem to quickly learn by observing or unconsciously following the role modelling of their society that they can get their own way when using this attitudinal style. It is clear to them that there are benefits. They get special attention, and people appease and please them. Their needs are met, they are not worried about yours, and they say what happens, when and how.

There are many benefits to having an intimate partner whom the controlling person can shape to meet their needs rather than having to put in the higher-order thinking required to compromise and collaborate. Life is so much easier for them. They can make choices for themselves only. They occasionally use a timely dose of generosity to avoid an uprising against themselves, however, their attitude towards their intimate partners and children is unwise and limited.

People with this attitudinal style are difficult (if not impossible) and scary to communicate and live with. They raise the trauma level of people around them.

Conversational Control at the Highest Level

At the highest level of the continuum, the abuser has a fixed superior, entitled and adversarial attitude towards their intimate partner. They target their partner with a system of tactics to gain and maintain the upper hand.

A person with this fixed SEA attitudinal style creates a pattern of Conversational Control so thick and strong that the relationship is coercive. At its basis, when we are being coerced, there is a process of others 'forcing' their own way on us, by words and by behaviours, rather than entering into a process of discussion to reach a mutual agreement (that's right, the Middle Column!). A fixed SEA attitudinal style can be very dangerous.

These are the sorts of things that clients might say to me about how the attitudinal style of their partner/ex-partner feels:

- Superior 'I govern you'

- We are not equals.
- There is no equal playing field.
- I am not a person to them.
- They are on a pedestal.
- I am a servant, slave, a worker.
- They think I belong to them.
- They are in charge.

- Entitled 'You serve me'

- Their expectations are my guiding light.
- I have to conform to their standards, needs and wants.
- I do all the adapting and the compromising.
- There are rules, and they can change every day.

- Adversarial 'I will always win and be right'

- They always win, I always lose.
- It's never going to be relevant to them so why waste my breath.
- They are competitive, not collaborative.
- If I stop feeding their needs the relationship gets worse.

The combination of a fixed, win/lose mindset and high levels of Conversational Control in a relationship creates two serious problems. First, there is no actual 'relationship'; it is an arrangement, and the arrangement is only to one person's benefit. Second, it can't be 'repaired', with therapy or counselling. That's because the attitudinal style behind higher levels of Conversational Control is too resistant to change.

A Jigsaw Puzzle

The diagram below represents how a SEA attitudinal style is at the core of a coercive relationship. It will play out and show up in the way you are treated in every area of the relationship. The jigsaw pieces interlock as any jigsaw puzzle does. **An essential part of the puzzle is that whatever happens in one area of the relationship affects every other area.** It is often overlooked that everything that happens, every piece of the jigsaw puzzle, is interlinked and interrelated.

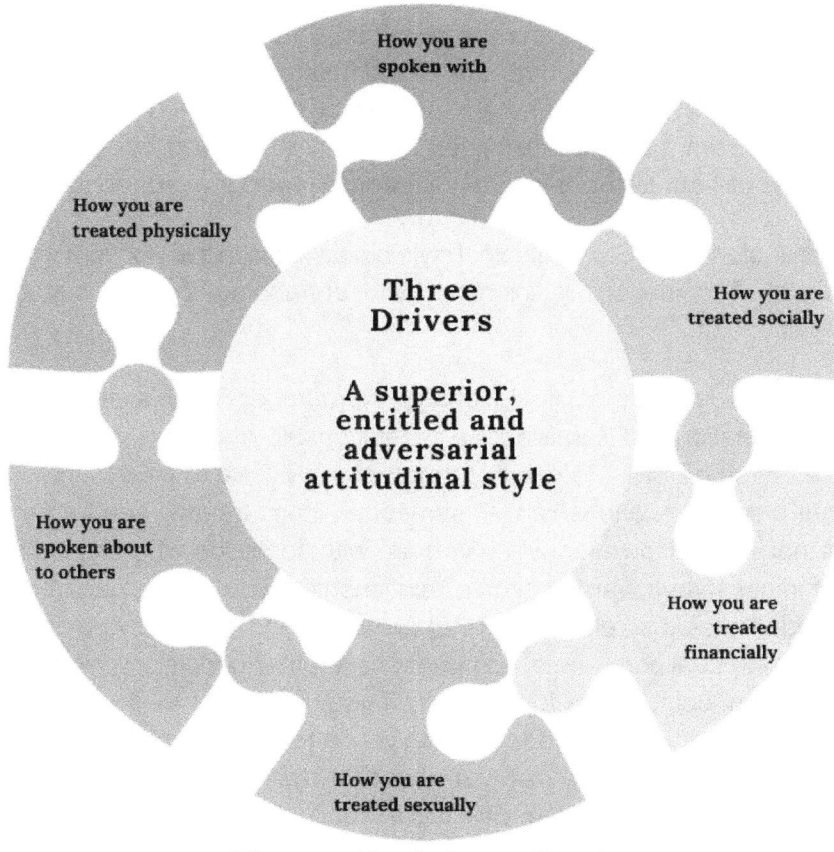

Diagram 10 - A Jigsaw Puzzle

The Jigsaw Pieces

Let's take social arrangements. Someone with a SEA attitudinal style will create tension around who you are friends with, who you relate with, when, and why. Your hobbies might be under so much scrutiny and comment that you can't enjoy them, so you give them up. It might be hard for you when you are out together as they could ignore you, put you down, interrogate you for appearing to flirt, and generally act like a disrespectful boss towards you rather than your partner. Being treated like that as a pattern will infiltrate every other area of the relationship.

Consider this treatment overlapping with how you're treated financially by this person. The conversations around money would be a system of Arcing Up and Down tactics used by your partner to shut you down, avoid, override or intimidate you. This means you will either not know about the finances because you'll be kept in the dark, you will be made to do all the work and hand over all your money, or you will be financially micromanaged and supervised.

It will all start in the SEA attitudinal style but continue in the Conversational Control. This pattern is insidious and entrapping, but it's just the beginning.

Let's consider the sexual relationship. Remember Sarah's story of her sexual relationship with Mark? Any relationship may have a worse or different story. Still, the result is that it is oppressive to be expected to have a sexual relationship with someone who is treating you as if you are not equal. However, when you are with someone who has a SEA attitudinal style towards intimate relationships, you will be required to provide the sexual relationship that they want and not what would work for you. Sexual comments, comparisons to other people, expectations to perform, being made to feel guilty if you don't want to, pushing you into sexual activities that don't please you, and sensing retaliation if you don't comply. This is all sexual abuse. It may not be violent in the physical sense of the word. Still, it is sexually disrespectful, and hardly what would happen in a more equal relationship.

The attitudinal style and the way you are spoken to is like the glue that binds the puzzle.

Compare How You Are Being Treated in Every Area of Your Relationship

This type of relationship is a whole different ball game from the lower levels of Conversational Control. The SEA attitudinal style creates a higher level of Conversational Control rather than occasional or issue-based control.

If I focus on each jigsaw piece of the diagram and ask clients how they were treated in that area of the relationship, we can build a clear picture of how the relationship functions. It doesn't take a counsellor to do this. We can ask ourselves. The trick is to compare what is happening and how you are being treated to what would happen if you felt safe and connected in each area of the relationship. We forget to do that and it can take other people to remind us how an equal relationship would look and feel in every aspect, what all the conversations and discussions would sound and feel like, and what would likely be the difference in the issues they face.

Are They Abusive, Narcissistic, or Both?

People described as abusive, toxic, or narcissistic are likely to have a superior, entitled, and adversarial attitude towards their intimate partners yet may treat their own friends, colleagues and family in a completely different way.

Take Sally, for example. 'My friends and neighbours all thought my husband [Mark] was wonderful. He went everywhere to offer help and was very charismatic. He told me I looked unfriendly and he told everyone I was the problem. They treated me warily, and he'd say it was my fault for looking so unfriendly. But he was running me down to others in my community all along. He would tell our neighbours…she is not well.'

Someone actually diagnosed as a psychopath, sociopath, or with narcissistic personality disorder, however, will more likely have this attitude towards anyone they interact with, even those they are using to assist their cause. This means other people will be negatively affected by their attitudinal style and behaviours, not just their intimate partner.

When it comes to Coercive Control, people will have and use this attitude towards their intimate partner, and can behave quite differently towards others, depending on the type of Coercive Control they use. How often do we hear, 'They are so lovely to everyone else'? This can make it very difficult to determine what is happening. Some people who use Coercive Control can be more charismatic than others. Others are less likeable and socially less well responded to.

Everyone thought Mark was a great team player, supportive and fun. Sarah felt humiliated and confused watching him having a good time and responding kindly to others at social or family events. It was a very deep wound that she carried, so deep she could not share it with anybody. Imagine being the scapegoat of someone so well-loved or revered. It is an impossible situation to be in and one often cultivated by those with a superior, entitled and adversarial attitudinal style.

Let's think about dictators, tyranny, and oppression in countries and organisations. It is easy to see that dictators feel superior, consider themselves entitled, and will be adversarial, especially to any resistance to their rule. Unfortunately, this attitude is common among politicians, world leaders, and those who wield great power over others. The history of the world seems full of examples of how this attitudinal style has created war, oppression, and communication between countries that doesn't even vaguely resemble what is possible in the Middle Column!

The way that women are treated in some countries, as though they are less than and have fewer or no rights, is a clear example of this attitudinal style at work. Men in these countries regard themselves as superior and entitled, so they will dictate what the women are able and not able to do or say. Any resistance is met with an adversarial attitude that can put the woman at greater physical and psychological risk than she is already in. The Response Framework is unlikely to work to make any shifts in the relationship; it can only be used to stay psychologically saner and more independent, even if forced into obedience.

Historically, in white culture and Western societies, it has been the male gender that dictates social mores, the legal system, and who and what is important. However, this book is not about gender because although social norms have created and perpetuated gender inequality, any person of any gender can use Conversational Control. It happens everywhere: in the schoolyard, the workplace, behind closed doors, on our TV and film screens, in politics, and between friends, relatives, groups, and countries. Creating Conversational Equality does not seem to be a popular goal to strive for. So, in our relationships, it is no wonder that it is difficult for us to recognise and respond to Unfair Conversational Tactics in a way that encourages a return to the Middle Column. This is what I meant about humanity not having good conversational role models.

To complicate matters, a SEA attitudinal style can be expressed differently. Even though the same attitudinal core exists, people will use a pattern of Arcing Up and Down tactics consistent with what they are invested in, their personality and interests, and what they like to control. This is especially obvious in intimate relationships. Coercive Controllers express these attitudes by using different Conversational Control patterns. For example, some are very focused on sexual obedience, and their conversations reflect this. In contrast, others focus more on other forms of obedience and control, such as financial, social, how the household is run, the noise level they'll accept, or what they think is appropriate for you to wear, think, feel, or do.

Let's unpack what a SEA attitudinal style creates in any relationship and how it plays out in an intimate relationship. The high level of

Conversational Control means we cannot be heard or have equal input into the decisions, arrangements, and plans, which we would have in an equal relationship.

We will see there are many types of Double Standards that we are subjected to. These deny you a fair and equal exchange, essentially saying, 'You must accommodate me, but I don't have to do the same for you.' Double Standards are, at their basis, emotionally abusive and create other forms of abuse such as social, sexual, financial, physical, verbal, psychological and cultural.

The higher the level of Conversational Control, the thicker the web of Double Standards. At lower levels, there can be the occasional Double Standards, which can easily be resolved once they are pointed out. However, Double Standards that result from superior, entitled, and adversarial attitudes create extreme inequality and prevent Relational Justice. That is because this attitudinal style will set us up to accommodate, adjust, and adapt to the other person.

There is often an 'or else' quality to a Double Standard. There will be retaliation if you don't submit or cater. There are Double Standards that deny us the same rights, deny us reciprocity or mutual and fair exchanges, and deny us accountability, as no responsibility is ever truly accepted. There will be a thick tangle of them within which no one can survive without there being negative effects on their emotional and mental health. Once we can name a Double Standard, though, it can lose its hold over us.

Here are some examples of Double Standards from my counselling room:

> 'Working out all the Double Standards in my relationship took me a long time. There was such a high level of Conversational Control that I stopped being able to see the forest for the trees. Some of them were so subtle. Anyway, who wants to spend their time working these things out? I wasn't in a relationship for that. But now I know why I had a nervous breakdown. In my

relationship, they told me what we could discuss and when. I didn't have that right. They acted like they were the gold standard, that only they knew how to do it right. Apparently, they were an expert on my life as well as theirs. I was not. I had to understand them and fit in around them. They didn't return this. They felt entitled to use but did not accept blame, criticism, or analysis. Their feelings were more important than mine. I was willing to compromise, and it took me a while to realise they wouldn't. I had to account for my time, they didn't. I was expected to be sexually available, regardless of my own desires or emotions. He labelled me as selfish if I sought time, friendships, or resources for myself, but he freely pursued what he wanted. I had to always consider his approval of my actions, yet he never sought my approval of his actions.'

When we are in a relationship of any sort, we can't always zoom out far enough to take in such things as the extent or amount of Double Standards we are being governed by. In higher levels of Conversational Control, there will be so many Double Standards, that they will usually be outside our awareness. We might be able to detect some but not others. If we were to recognise one and point it out, we would receive an adversarial, argumentative response. This means there will not be a fair conversation, but we will be treated to a cleverly arranged array of Arcing Up and Down tactics. The aim will be to either silence or threaten us into submission, or to convince and confuse us (gaslighting) that the Double Standard doesn't exist or is there because of a fault in us. A superior, entitled, and adversarial attitudinal style allows no real discussion or equality. Even in times of relative harmony within the relationship, the Double Standards still exist.

We will also be trapped within Double Binds, where we are 'damned if we do and damned if we don't'. Double binds are unfair and illogical expectations of us that are also contradictory. If we experience Conversational Control, there will be Double Binds we are trapped within that will affect our health, well-being, and rights. The higher the level of Conversational Control we are experiencing, the more Double Binds there will be. But once we can name a Double Bind, we are more able to be free of it, as we will no longer waste energy trying to solve the riddle that Double Binds create. There is no answer except not to accept the challenge!

These Double Binds are emotionally abusive and can create great anguish and distress (like they did for me with the story of my fifth-grade teacher, Mrs B). Not only are they unsolvable, but they are coercive. For example, situations are made 'unwinnable' by requesting something of us, like speaking up in the relationship, but then describing us as overbearing when we try to comply.

Below are examples of Double Binds from Sally, Hayley and Sam. Neither experienced physical violence, but they experienced very high levels of Conversational Control and Coercive Control. It was impossible to hold their partners accountable, work out what would gain their partner's respect, or how to prevent further emotional abuse.

> 'He thought I should be more assertive and encouraged me to do an assertiveness course. So I did. He didn't like it. So, then he would say, "Forget about this assertiveness, you are being overbearing," and he would be angry with me. He wanted a life in the country, so we moved. Then he started to say, "Sally, I really want you to be a real woman, to have a flat in town where you just push a button to warm it rather than having to light a fire." I said, "You know I love this lifestyle. What are you on about?" He replied, "You can't be a real woman out here," and he wanted a real woman. Yes, I couldn't win, I wasn't assertive enough, then I was overbearing, and when I had moved out into the country as he wanted, then I wasn't a real woman. Yes, that did hurt.' (Sally)

> 'He wouldn't give me any money but didn't want me to work He would justify it by saying that a woman's place was in the home, that I was neglecting my family and my duties. I went out to work because he never gave me enough

money for the children or to run the household. So, I had to get to work, work, race home, get the dinner ready for him and his children and our baby, and go back to work. Yet, he used to work from home.' (Hayley)

'I understood there were double standards but I had no idea how many Double Binds there were in my relationship. I tried so hard to make it work, but it was impossible. I know that now. My partner told me I was either too quiet or too boring in conversations but that I was attracting too much attention to myself when engaging with people. If that had been the only Double Bind, I might have caught on and challenged it. But there were more. If I didn't want to listen to their monologues, it meant I didn't love them, so I would have to listen to what a bad partner I was. If I disagreed with them, I was mistreating them. Eventually, I stopped talking to them, as there was no point in it, so then they accused me of being secretive. If I said I was hurt at how I felt treated, I was blamed for being hurt. In the end, they said they wouldn't have needed to go behind my back if I had met their needs.' (Sam)

There will be violations of the human rights and boundaries that we would expect to have in an equal relationship. We have a set of universal rights and a set of individual boundaries that protect our humanity, and the difference between where the other person ends and where we begin is clear. In a situation with high-level control, our universal rights to an equal voice, physical safety and independence, financial honesty, sexual respect, and privacy will not be honoured; the extent to which will depend upon the style of the Coercive Controller.

Our boundaries are the things that define who we are and what behaviours are acceptable to us. They can be physical (don't touch me like that) or emotional (be truthful). A fixed superior, entitled and adversarial attitude towards us means we will have our rights and boundaries routinely ignored, thwarted, or overridden.

When our rights and boundaries are recognised, we have a relationship with Conversational Equality. The diagram below explains our rights in each of the main domains of a relationship.

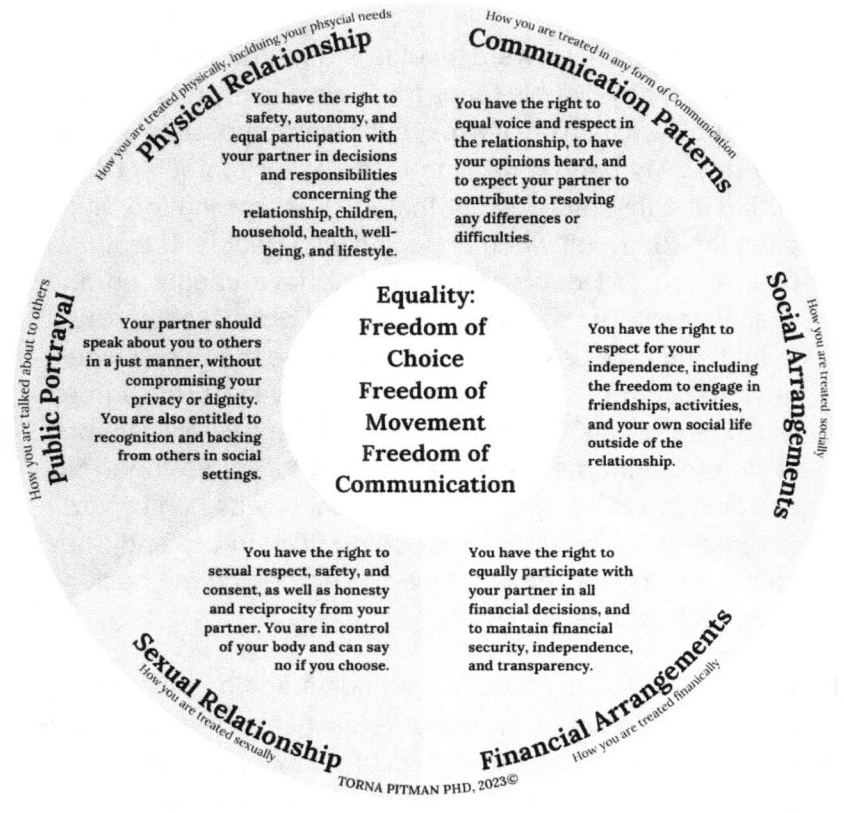

Diagram 11 - Our Rights

Kit's Story – Compare Kit's story to what her rights should have been:

Kit would wake up at night and find that her partner was pushing himself upon her. She objected, and his comeback was that if she wasn't going to be a good sexual partner for him, he would have to look elsewhere. Then he would ask her where else she was getting it and accuse her of having an affair. In the middle of the night, this was exhausting and debilitating, and eventually, Kit learned to comply so as not to upset him; she felt obligated and a bit afraid of what would happen if she didn't. Giving in also meant she could get back to sleep to deal with the busy day ahead. Her partner left most of the responsibilities with their baby to her. Kit bore the guilt her partner gave her that she was not a good, enthusiastic sexual partner. It didn't occur to her whether her partner was meeting her own sexual needs or that he was not being sexually respectful. Kit was being subjugated. She felt far too guilty, tired, and confused to zoom out and see the bigger picture.

Kit's partner had a superior, entitled, and adversarial attitude, so he treated Kit poorly in every area of the relationship, not just sexually. Financially, Kit was not allowed to access their money and had to rely on her partner for housekeeping money. She had to use her small inheritance to fund herself where this fell short. He would not give her money to buy food or nappies, there was no joint account, and she was not allowed to use his credit card. She experienced being lied to and having assets hidden from her. Kit was being financially abused and exploited.

Socially, he knew what kind of remarks would get a certain effect, so he would provoke and wind her up before arriving at friends' houses, or if they had visitors, so that she could not enjoy herself. He also made sure they lived in a place with little transport; as he worked, his social life was fine, and he had the car. Kit was being socially abused and isolated.

Physically, Kit was not allowed certain medications, to put on weight, and was not allowed contraception (this is reproductive control). He would stand over her, yell at her, stabbing at her with his finger. Kit was being physically abused and threatened.

However, to cap it all off, he was defaming Kit to his friends, family, and workplace as a needy, sulky, insecure woman who just couldn't get her act together and was never happy. She 'just needed to find an activity that she enjoyed doing'. Kit was experiencing defamation abuse and was alienated.

It is a confusing situation to be caught in, profoundly affecting our quality of life. Imagine how Kit got through each day trapped within these Double Standards, Double Binds, and violations of her rights and boundaries. Kit was experiencing high levels of Conversational Control, as well as emotional, verbal, psychological, sexual, physical, social, financial, and defamation abuse. This is Coercive Control.

If Kit were able to have a conversation with her partner within the Middle Column, this would not happen. Her partner would not want or be able to mould and groom her into such unfair subservience. He would not have a SEA attitudinal style, so even though there could be bumpy, argumentative moments within the relationship, it would have a good chance of being equal.

Six Commonly Asked Questions About Conversational Control

These questions are often asked of me by people who have experienced higher levels of Conversational Control and abuse in their relationships and need to understand how it came about:

1. Is it about anger?

The anger of a Coercive Controller is not based on healthy boundaries. It is based on unfair, oppressive expectations. Remember, their expectations of you are unfair, irrational, and contradictory. They are invading your boundaries and installing their own government in your life. Their anger is based on their expectation that you will comply with this. It is abusive anger. You are not violating their healthy boundaries! Physical violence, for example, is not necessarily the outcome of a build-up of tension or angry altercations. It can be premeditated, or random without any build-up or rationale.

2. Doesn't it take two to tango?

Not when there is abuse or Coercive Control. It is entirely one-sided. The idea of 'it takes two' may apply to an equal relationship, where there is a level playing field, but not when there is misuse and abuse of power.

3. Am I codependent?

That is an unfair and inaccurate victim blaming term. Coercive Control is abuse. You are groomed, abused and traumatised, not codependent.

4. Is it about mental health, stress, or alcohol?

No, it isn't. These factors can increase the severity, volatility, intensity, and drama of incidents and provide explanations or excuses. However, mental health, stress or alcohol do not explain the pattern of attitudes and behaviours that were there before any incident and after any incident, and will still be there even when their mental health, stress or alcohol problems are addressed. It is hard to come to terms with that when you are hoping treatment will change the dynamic.

5. Is it about their trauma?

Trauma can increase the severity of incidents but again, trauma does not create the pattern of behaviour that springs from a superior, entitled, and adversarial attitudinal style. Past trauma is no excuse for being abusive. We can all learn new skills despite our trauma. I have seen people talk about their trauma as if it explains and excuses their current behaviour. Yet, their partner, whom they abuse, has experienced worse trauma than they have and has not developed a pattern of relating and behaving that is abusive. It's not okay that people think their traumatic background explains, allows, and excuses them for disrespectful, unfair communication. I hear this as an excuse all the time. 'They had a traumatic background/terrible childhood.' Even someone with significant trauma who communicates poorly can still get into the Middle Column and have a decent conversation. Having a traumatic background doesn't excuse us from recognising the impact we can have on people when we are out of sorts. We can still make amends. The amends have to stay made, though. In other words, what was amended actually stays amended. An apology must have substance.

6. Why didn't I see this in the beginning?

It isn't always possible to see it at the beginning. Many boundary violations can be outside of our awareness or experience. There are not necessarily any obvious red flags. The start of the relationship often shows great promise of equality and intimacy. The red flags show only after you commit more, such as moving in together, getting married, or having a child. All of which require greater interdependence. There may have been no initial love bombing or rushing you into a relationship. The idea that there are always red flags and we simply miss them is not true. It emphasises that we can avoid certain people because there will be red flags but does not acknowledge the slow, insidious conversational grooming process that we can all be fooled by and can't necessarily detect initially. We need to understand the Conversational Control and grooming process, which will give us the greatest chance to avoid being trapped.

In Summary

Where there are higher levels of Conversational Control, our rights and boundaries are at risk. It creates anxiety because the atmosphere is more hostile. We hesitate to discuss, ask, debate, or negotiate about a topic. If we do, we experience any variety of Unfair Conversational Tactics that naturally makes us feel some level or nuance of anxiety, fear, obligation, guilt, shame or confusion rather than the space for individual opinions and alternate points of view. If we stand up for ourselves, we will be retaliated against with more Conversational Tactics. There is a lack of empathy and a focus on putting us back in 'our place', which is to be more amenable. It is a never-ending cycle that can be very covert and quiet, or loud and overtly intimidating. We all need to know that there may be red flags, but there are conversational tendencies that you are more likely to pick up on if you know what to look for.

The next chapter describes the conversational tendencies that you must watch for as signs of someone likely to be controlling you rather than connecting with you.

7

Untangling Themes in Conversations

How we are spoken to affects us to the point that we can be slowly but surely encouraged, trained, or groomed to think, feel, believe, and act a certain way. This can be positive or negative. So, it is critical in any relationship, whether intimate or not, to consider how we impact and are impacted by conversational patterns.

As a social worker and counsellor, I have talked with many older people, some at the end stages of their life. A recurrent theme is the conversations they have had or wished they had had with certain people. They tell me about the conversations they avoided or refused to have and their deep regrets about how that impacted the other person and their relationship with them. I hear so much about the conversations that worked and the ones that didn't. The attitude we project, the set of our muscles, what we do with our body whilst we speak or listen, and the words we use work towards building or breaking that connection. I know that I was not always aware of the impact of my own conversational style, and my life could have been much smoother in places if I had a greater ability to detect Unfair Conversational Tactics from a young age and had a framework to use to make sense of it or respond.

Our Rights

It's helpful to remember that we all have rights in conversations. Individuals have the right to engage in a productive conversation where they have the opportunity to clarify, explore, discuss, and disagree. They also have the right to a negotiating and collaborative discussion that aims to achieve a win/win resolution, with mutual decisions, plans, arrangements, or agreements being made. Different perspectives should be acknowledged and respected, and individuals should be heard and then responded to. The provision of adequate detail and information, along with keeping the conversation on track, is essential. Furthermore, individuals have the right to a fair, safe, and equal discussion, including the possibility of receiving an apology if necessary, and ensuring a proper conclusion to the discussion, promoting Conversational Equality.

It can make relationships easier when we know our rights to understand and insist on a conversation where both people put effort into the following so that the conversation remains in the Middle Column. This is a handy list of the rights you should expect in a conversation:

- **It feels emotionally safe**: Participants express their thoughts and feelings without fear of judgment or reprisal.
- **There is an emphasis on equal speaking**: Both parties can speak and contribute to the conversation without dominating or shutting the other down.
- **It feels collaborative**: The conversation is marked by a collaborative spirit where individuals work together to find common ground and mutual solutions.
- **It feels respectful**: The tone of the conversation is respectful, and participants avoid using adversarial or condescending language.
- **We feel heard**: People actively listen to each other's perspectives, seek to understand, and respond thoughtfully.

- **There is shared decision-making**: Decisions and solutions are reached through a shared process, and both parties have input into the outcomes.
- **There are proper apologies and amends**: If disagreements or misunderstandings exist, individuals are willing to make an apology of substance and make amends for any hurtful behaviour.
- **There is a focus on solutions**: Rather than avoiding or deflecting issues, or trying to make someone wrong, there is a genuine effort to address problems and find practical solutions.
- **There is a drive towards mutual understanding**: There is a sense of being on the same team, with participants acknowledging each other's viewpoints and working towards a common understanding.
- **There is relational growth**: The conversation contributes to the growth and evolution of the relationship, fostering a sense of goodwill and connection.

If these elements are present, the conversation is respectful of each other's rights and is therefore in the Middle Column. Conversely, if the conversation lacks these qualities and is marked by Arcing Up and Arcing Down tactics, it has moved away from the Middle Column.

That doesn't mean the conversation can't be directed back towards the Middle Column. We can't sanitise all conversations, as we are human and can act out in frustration and anxiety. Still, if we respond to a request to get back into the Middle Column or can get ourselves back into the Middle Column, then the conversation can continue in a healthier way.

Questions I Ask in the Counselling Room

If you know what to look for, it is very simple to work out who is controlling the conversations and to what extent, and who is reacting, struggling, and getting blamed for being the problem. It is easy for a counsellor to get the wrong end of the stick if they do not ask what happens in the couple's everyday conversations.

As a counsellor, I notice that people describe the faults they see in their partner's personality and actions. However, rather than attribute their issues to trauma, the need for anger management, family of origin issues, stress, mental health, or alcohol issues, I want to know if there are low or high levels of Conversational Control. Otherwise, we can keep going around in circles. I will redirect the focus and ask some variation of the following types of questions about the conversations in their relationship, because that's where the problem usually lies:

- How do the conversations tend to go?
- Are there issues or areas where the conversations work better?
- What makes the difference, do you think?
- Would you say there are shared arrangements, agreements, and decisions in the relationship?
- Are there any conversations that haven't been had, weren't finished, or didn't work well that still impact you?
- How do you let each other know what you need?
- How would you describe the level of safety or emotional companionship?
- What would be your ideal sort of conversation with them?
- What can you, can't you, and would you like to discuss?
- How would you describe the consequences of what you can't discuss?

The answers they give me (I ask the couple in separate sessions rather than together) tell me a lot about how the dynamics work between them and if there is an equal playing field. We can all ask ourselves the same questions if we feel worried about a relationship. When we focus on what can and can't be talked about and why, it is very revealing.

The 'why' may be fear, and then we have to ask ourselves, fear of what? How bad will it be? A strong reaction? A tantrum? Of being blamed and shamed for daring to raise it? Retaliation? Punishment? If we are afraid, isolating exactly why can be difficult but very revealing, and it will tell you a lot about the level of connection or control in the relationship.

The Stranglehold of High-Level Conversational Control

A higher level of Conversational Control means that there will be a fixed pattern of relating that creates a stranglehold on the other person. Maintaining our independence and ability to influence, make changes, or achieve equality in the relationship is impossible. This is how the stranglehold works from the controller's perspective:

> 'I prefer to win and be right. At my worst, I prefer to win and you to lose. I see conflict as all your fault in general. I believe I am superior and, therefore, entitled to call the shots and arrange you and the relationship to my liking. I am adversarial, oppositional, and neglectful of you. I may not be obviously abusive, but I set the standards. I know how to engage your sympathy and hope, so I am intermittently kind, charming, vulnerable, and endearing, and you confuse that with emotional intimacy.
>
> 'If you look carefully, you will see that my entitlement creates expectations of you that are full of Double Standards. One standard for me, another for you. I expect you to compromise, but I won't. You can be assured that I will hold you to a higher standard than I do for myself. Your behaviour, thoughts, ideas, hopes, and dreams are up for question, whereas mine are not.
>
> 'You will also see that I trap you in Double Binds, where you cannot resolve the dilemmas that I put you in. For example, I expect you to revolve around me but not depend on me. Another routine dilemma for you will be that I will hurt you in some way and then blame you for being hurt. You won't fully

understand why you feel distressed because I keep you fairly busy, so you can't see the bigger picture of the tangle my attitudes and words weave for you. I will not seem to notice nor really care if I violate your rights and boundaries.

'I use a high-level pattern of Conversational Control to dismantle any discussion you attempt to have with me. If you stand up to me, I will consider you out of line and retaliate against you to ensure you stay more in line. I lack empathy for the situations I put you in and how you will come off second best. I am pretty blind to the impact of my behaviour on the quality of your life. I like to use your resources and services, and I expect you to accommodate me while I do that.'

Understanding this stranglehold is important so you are never at the mercy of someone's superior, entitled, and adversarial attitude. It is impossible to redirect a conversation towards the Middle Column at higher levels because this attitude does not value what the Middle Column offers, and this creates the stranglehold on the relationship dynamics.

What the Karlys of the World Want

Most of the Karlys that I interviewed or counselled value the Middle Column:

'I used to really work on how if I change my words, if I present them in a certain way, he won't be able to help but understand. He will see what I mean. I'm sure it'll make sense to him, and he'll hear what I've got to say. You know, even when I did that, I'd still come out of it saying, 'Yes, you're right, I am sorry." I can remember doing it and hearing myself saying, 'Yeah, I am sorry I brought it up. I am sorry I said that.' How did I feel like my opinions were so right ten minutes ago, but now I feel like I am out of order? You are not entitled to say, "I don't like this," so, you just can't win...'

They do not consider themselves expert communicators nor do they have a SEA attitudinal style towards their partner.

> 'I prefer there to be a win/win. I will try hard to make it right and to connect with you. I have empathy. I want emotional companionship. With a win/lose person, I can lose my bearings and have trauma reactions, negative thoughts, and shame. I can end up lacking autonomy, agency, or equality because I am easily encouraged, trained, or groomed to avoid your distress, disappointment, disapproval, or disgust.

> 'I walk on eggshells to keep it okay for you, and I feel trapped, which results in a decline in my mental, emotional, and physical health. I often end up with less status, money, and opportunities. I feel confused, a lack of fairness or justice, and like a second-class citizen. Is it my fault? Did I do something wrong? I usually end up feeling confused, depressed, angry, anxious, sad, and in pain.'

Recognising Themes and Tactics of Conversational Control

I often think if there is enough goodwill, people who are having difficulty coping with certain conversations or issues will pull themselves out of reactivity back into the Middle Column given half a chance and an invitation to do so – as long as they don't have a fixed superior, entitled and adversarial stance.

But when someone is more than just a poor communicator and habitually controls a conversation, they will strategically and cleverly switch from one tactic to another. This means:

- Switching from one Arcing Up tactic to another Arcing Up tactic.
- Switching from one Arcing Down tactic to another Arcing Down tactic.
- Switching between an Arcing Up to an Arcing Down tactic or vice versa.

Sometimes, I watch or listen in fascination as this switching is played out between people. I see it on the TV screen; I have experienced it face-to-face and heard it on the phone in a difficult conversation. Not only do I listen and observe the pattern of tactics used to throw the conversation off course, but I also take note of the *theme* underlying their choice of Unfair Conversational Tactics.

I saw these themes come up time and time again in my research and practice, and my thinking was further influenced by a great article written by Michael Flood, Molly Dragiewicz, and Bob Pease in 2018 on backlash and resistance to gender equality. (Listed in resources.)

Knowing these themes can help us disengage from the effect of tactics used against us and consider our options for responding. We can see that people often unconsciously use set patterns in conversations. Those who use more high-level Conversational Control are more strategic and will use particular tactics and themes that make it easier to train, groom, and encourage people to respond how they want.

The 11 Themes That Control a Conversation

Here are the themes that can be routinely used in any combination to control a conversation:

1. Not interested in the issue: (disengaged, unreceptive, withholding, sulking, irrelevant, evasive, confusing responses)

Emma: 'I've noticed we've been having trouble really talking lately.'
Ryan: 'Can't we just chill?'

2. Doesn't think there is an issue: (withholding, deciding what can and can't be discussed)

Emma: 'I feel like we're not clicking in our conversations.'
Ryan: 'Nah, you're overthinking it. Anyway, we don't always need to click.'

3. Reactive because an issue has been raised: (bristling, blaming, intimidating, groaning, leaves the room, sarcasm)

Emma: 'Can we work on being more open when we talk?'
Ryan (defensively): 'Oh God, why are you bringing this up now? We were doing fine before you started stressing about it.'

4. Blames the issue on the person affected: (accusations, fixating, name-calling, twisting, sarcasm, triangulating, lying, point scoring, ridicule, sneering, distorting)

Emma: 'We need to figure out why we're not connecting when we talk.'
Ryan: 'This is your thing; you're always overanalysing and making it a big deal. Where are you on your cycle?'

5. Attacks the validity of the issue: (denying, ridiculing, joking, sneering, mimicking, distorting, questioning, interrogating)

Emma: 'Our talks feel off lately.'
Ryan: 'I can't believe how focused you are on "our talk". Who cares about talk?'

6. Attacks the credibility of the person affected: (defining you, defaming you, putting you down, blaming and shaming you)

Emma: 'I've been feeling ignored during our conversations.'
Ryan: 'Come on, you exaggerate these things. You don't know what you are talking about. You've always done this. It is exhausting; why do you do it? What is wrong with you? You need some counselling. It's not like I'm deliberately ignoring you.'

7. Reverses the issue so that they are the victim: (poor me, self-pity, wounded, distorting)

Emma: 'Let's work on our communication issues.'
Ryan: 'I can't believe you're putting all of this onto me. I'm the one who's feeling misunderstood here.'

8. Undermines you and the issue: (trivialises, minimises, interrupts, monologues, decides what is or isn't important, tries to catch you out, threatening)

Emma: 'Can we talk about how we communicate, please?'
Ryan: 'I don't have the same amount of time as you to do navel-gazing and go round in circles.'

9. Complicates the issue: (circular conversation, psychobabble, defining, analysing, gaslighting, interrogating, twisting your motives, finger pointing; fixes, amends, improves, or critiques what you say)

Emma: 'I want us to understand each other better.'
Ryan: 'Maybe the problem is that we're both wired differently. I think you just want me to be more like you, and I am different. It's not as simple as just talking more. Why can't you just accept me as I am?'

10. Brings up another issue: (deflecting, changing the topic, pointing the finger)

Emma: 'We need to work on our communication.'
Ryan: 'And what about your habit of leaving things everywhere? We should talk about that too.'

11. Refuses to resolve the issue: (shuts down, evades, bored, tired, indifferent)

Emma: 'Can we find a way to communicate more effectively?'
Ryan: 'I'm not interested, I'm too tired, and I don't care.'

This diagram sums the themes up:

TANGLED WEB OF WORDS

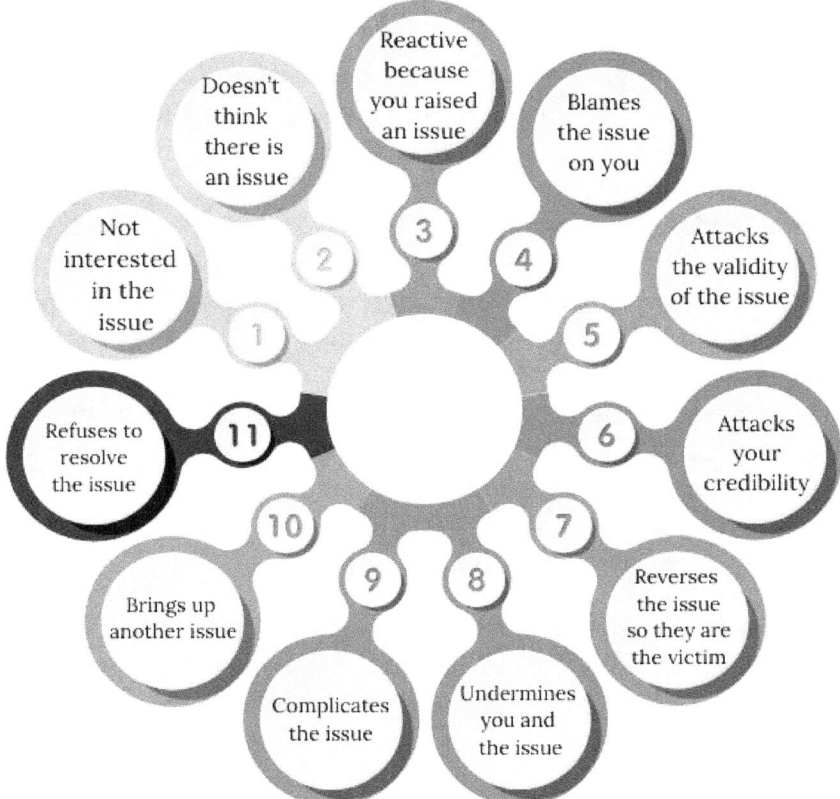

Diagram 12 - Conversational Themes

Remember, we can all use these ways of mishandling an issue that someone else is trying to raise with us. It doesn't mean we are a narcissist or that we are a problem. It means that we forced that particular conversation to a standstill. It couldn't work. We can do this to each other occasionally, but we can also rectify it if someone points it out to us.

If we use a high-level of conversational control, though, and we have a superior, entitled, and adversarial attitudinal style to intimate relationships and maybe any relationship, we are much more adept at ignoring, neglecting, sidestepping, evading, obstructing, or overpowering any attempts made to have a conversation in the Middle Column than we are at having an equal, fair conversation.

Emotional and Psychological Abuse

When we are up against high-level Conversational Control, we will be unable to see all the themes, tactics, Double Standards, and Double Binds we are subjected to. We can't see or make sense of the conversational tangle that we experience. We don't have the training, and no one has taught us. It is like we are a rank beginner tennis player up against a highly trained professional world-class tennis player who has a win/lose psychological mindset and is trained in all the tactics and strategies they can use to win as often as possible. They have no qualms about watching for your weaker areas and when and how to outsmart you. In a relationship, this attitudinal style towards conversations is emotionally and psychologically abusive, especially when it is a pattern. Treating a partner like an adversary you try to outsmart is okay on the tennis court but not in any relationship.

When we are routinely told who we are and what our motivations are, when we are analysed, put down, and spoken over the top of, when we are denied reassurance, comfort, connection, or clarification, this is *emotional abuse*.

When we are routinely treated as if our thinking, perception, memory, and intelligence are inferior, that is *psychological abuse*.

Usually, emotional and psychological abuse go hand in hand, and they both underlie all other forms of abuse in the relationship, such as physical, social, financial, verbal, sexual, technological, religious, parenting, and defamation.

Imagine dealing with someone who always has to have the last word and thinks they know everything about you. This person with a superior, entitled, and adversarial attitude tells you what you are, what you should do, and how you should feel. They're not interested in meeting you halfway or having an equal partnership. Instead, it's a constant cycle of them defining, defaming, and blaming you.

It is like they have a one-way lens; they look at you through this lens that determines whether they like what you are doing or saying and whether it is useful to them, and they feel entitled to use any unfair tactic to put you back in your place. They lack the capacity for a fair and balanced relationship. In their world, it's all about control, and they'll keep on dictating as they consider themselves the undisputed authority. It's like trying to converse with someone who refuses to see you as an equal partner and instead insists on being the sole director of the story. There isn't a relationship so much as there is an arrangement where, over time, you have had to assume a shape that works for them but cramps you into a much smaller version of yourself with fewer or no rights. This arrangement is unfair, unequal, and abusive.

You will hear a lot about yourself, but you will not hear any self-reflection, awareness of how they are thinking and behaving, and the assumptions they are making, or how they are deflecting from any accountability and refusing to consider their impact on you. They will 'police' you, acting more like your inspector, supervisor, manager, or boss rather than someone in an equal relationship with you. This is emotional and psychological abuse.

Examples of Emotional and Psychological Abuse

They will tell you:

1. **What you are**
   Example: 'You're lazy.'

2. **What you are doing**
   Example: 'You're spending too much time with friends.'

3. **How you feel**
   Example: 'You're never happy'

4. **How you are thinking**
   Example: 'You're not thinking logically.'

5. **What you need**
   Example: 'You need therapy.'

6. **What you want**
   Example: 'You just want someone to complain to.'

7. **What you should do**
   Example: 'You should follow my advice.'

8. **How you are**
   Example: 'You're too stubborn/thin/fat/lazy.'

9. **What you should know**
   Example: 'You should have known I would need that.'

10. **What's wrong with you**
    Example: 'You have always been oversensitive.'

11. **How your past affects you**
    Example: 'You are just like your mother.'

12. **What your future will be**
    Example: 'You will never be able to do that.'

13. **How you should take things**
    Example: 'You should just lighten up.'

14. **How you should behave**
    Example: 'You should be more fun.'

15. **What you should have**
    Example: 'You should have less revealing clothing.'

16. **What you should be like**
    Example: 'You should be more friendly.'

17. **What your perceptions are or should be**
    Example: 'You see it wrong.'

18. **How other people feel about you**
    Example: 'Others feel sorry for you.'

19. **What issues you can raise**
    Example: 'Not everyone has a memory like yours.'

Notice the emphasis on 'you' and the lack of emphasis on themself. If you dispute any of these put-downs, you will be spoken to with a combination of Unfair Conversational Tactics and themes to treat any issue or objection you raise.

For example, they will tell you about *you*, but never ask you or suggest anything remotely resembling the following:

- Can we take a moment to ensure we both feel okay emotionally in this conversation?
- What's your perspective? Let's find common ground where we both feel heard.
- How can we work together for a win/win outcome?
- Can you help me better understand your thoughts for a mutual solution?

Any form of conversation that is outside the Middle Column could be emotional or psychologically abusive, especially when it is a pattern. Many people have no idea that they are emotionally abusive when they deny you your rights to fair and equal conversations, and if they are at the lower end of the Conversational Control continuum, they will rectify it when it is pointed out to them.

Suppose they use a high level of Conversational Control and have a superior, entitled and adversarial stance towards others. In that case, they will readily and routinely use one of the eleven themes and a pattern of Arcing Up and Down to ruin a conversation and dispute anything you raise. Someone with this attitudinal style is not happy to reflect on their behaviour and, like the professional tennis player, will use any tactic, strategy, and manoeuvre to win over, run you around the court to dominate, exhaust, and outwit you.

Am I a Target or a Partner?

You become their target, not a partner. This is when you are trapped within the tangled web of dynamics created by their superior, entitled, and adversarial attitudinal style. You are targeted with high levels of Conversational Control, Double Standards, Double binds, and the possibility of retaliation if you don't comply with it all. When we are targeted, it is not about us. It is not about our personality or our 'problem areas'.

A really critical point I want you to understand is that personality issues, family of origin issues, past trauma or stress are only relevant when there is an equal playing field.

When you are a target, there is no equal playing field. Superior, entitled, and adversarial attitudes create a power imbalance and impossible dynamics. Your personality or any other issues you feel you have do not come into it. The Conversational Controller will undoubtedly use them to make you the problem, but that works only to deflect attention away from the unequal playing field created by the dynamics they have trapped you in. It is about what we are subjected to, how we are treated, and what makes the relationship impossible to thrive in, no matter what we do or try. It is also what makes a relationship dangerous.

When a partner uses higher levels of Conversational Control, they're taking away our ability to speak up and have a say in how our relationship functions. It's like being silenced and losing control over our lives and who we are. Anything from a quiet, calm, to a more intimidating pattern of Conversational Control can be used to watch, criticise, and restrict what we do, think, believe, or feel, how we dress, where we go, and what we are allowed or not allowed.

In our social life, being restricted can make us lose friends and support, leaving us alone and more vulnerable. Financially, not having equal input in the arrangements can make us feel insecure, dependent, taken advantage of, and like we have lost our independence. In our intimate relationship, not having an equal voice can ruin closeness and attraction, making us feel like a puppet, and exploited.

The complete absence of the Middle Column and the prevention of conversations that would happen there create a tangled web of words and dynamics, which are the direct opposite of Relational Justice, and that is Coercive Control. There doesn't have to be any physical violence. The emotional and psychological abuse will play out in every area of the relationship, not just part of it.

Coercive Control means that the target has their life ruled by their partner. It is very common but has not been well understood until recently, despite the attempts of targets and researchers to raise social, political, and legal awareness of it.

8

Untangling Agendas in Conversations

I have outlined how unfair and unequal conversations can develop into something more sinister, Coercive Control. Here is another way to explain how it works.

Let's imagine there are two countries, each with its own governments, lifestyles, cultures, languages, and rules. Each country has its own visa rules, and a passport is required to enter that country. The two countries do not bother each other as they do not share resources or need to negotiate boundary issues. Country A is looking to extend its influence and power worldwide and notices Country B for its rich mineral deposits and the possible labour force. It sends diplomats to the country and offers help for issues they have in return for access to some mineral deposits. As time passes, the diplomats from Country A begin to exert more and more control. At first, the offers of help from Country A seemed genuine, addressing some of the issues that Country B faced. But slowly and subtly, the diplomatic process shifts, becoming more controlling and manipulative.

With their superior and entitled attitude, Country A's diplomats start imposing their own lifestyle, culture, language, and rules onto the people of Country B. They disregard the customs and traditions of Country B's people, viewing them as inferior and needing 'civilising'.

Any objections raised by the people of Country B are met with adversarial responses from Country A's diplomats. They dismiss concerns, silence dissent, and use their influence to suppress opposition within Country B's government and society.

Gradually, Country A wheedles itself into the fabric of Country B, infiltrating its institutions and influencing its policies. With each passing day, Country B loses a little more of its autonomy and identity as Country A tightens its grip on the country.

Despite the initial promises of mutual benefit, the relationship between Country A and Country B became one of domination and control. The people of Country B found themselves trapped in a situation where their sovereignty was eroded, their cultural heritage was threatened, and the superior and entitled attitude of Country A silenced their voices. Ultimately, Country B became little more than a puppet state governed by Country A's interests and agenda.

This is exactly how a relationship that once held promise tips over into one where a colonising process is gradually taking place. The relationship usually feels confusing and tangled to the colonised partner, but really, there is a pattern where all the words and behaviours are linked to the superior, entitled, and adversarial attitudes at the core.

Colonising on an interpersonal level has many similarities to the colonising process that occurs internationally. The scale of abuse and the consequences cannot be compared to the destruction and damage to a country and its people; it is the themes that are similar. The mechanics of domination on an interpersonal scale resemble the mechanics of domination on an international scale.

Isabel and David's Story

Isabel and her partner, David, lived in a quiet suburb. With his education, status, charming demeanour and confident attitude, David believed himself superior to Isabel. He quietly viewed her as beneath him and felt entitled to control every aspect of her life.

David's adversarial attitude towards Isabel manifested in subtle yet manipulative ways. He would belittle her achievements, undermine her opinions, and dismiss her feelings. Isabel felt like she was walking on eggshells around David, afraid to express herself for fear of his anger and criticism.

David's Coercive Control extended way beyond emotional manipulation. He monitored Isabel's movements, checked her phone, and isolated her from her friends and family. He used threats and intimidation to keep her in line, creating a toxic dynamic of fear and submission in their relationship. He had a one-way focus on Isabel, expecting her to accommodate and adjust to him but providing no reciprocity. He certainly never held himself accountable for the sorts of situations that he put Isabel in. Isabel tried everything she knew to make it work without understanding the tangled web woven by David that she was stuck in. Her efforts were wasted as David made it impossible for their relationship to thrive, instead creating coercion and control that left Isabel feeling trapped and powerless, unable to break free from his suffocating grip.

Isabel started to doubt herself, lose confidence, and feel anxious. Anyone would. She monitored herself to avoid David's criticism. All this happened without her fully realising it. It was a slow process of adapting to David's training and grooming of her to change herself to suit him. Her level of fear was almost unconscious at first. Many targets do not realise how frightened they are and what they are afraid of. They also don't realise that changing themselves, although it is a normal response, does not change the relationship. You will never make enough or the right changes, because the expectations placed on you are usually completely illogical, contradictory and unjust. They do not deserve our efforts to accommodate them. We do try, though, until we have the support and information to get help and stay safe in the process.

If we think of Isabel as her own country with boundaries, including where she stopped and David started, David moved beyond interacting with her in a way that created healthy interdependence that also benefited Isobel. He inserted his government into her country and denied her the right to self-govern. Like Country A,

David saw the resources that Isabel could provide, such as labour, housekeeping, cooking, sexual services, financial support, child raising, and care. These were used by David to his own advantage. Like Country A, he did not reciprocate or give back, and never held himself accountable. David saw Isobel as Country B, a country he could annex to his own to increase his power, to govern and use all the resources while complaining and criticising why she did not seem to appreciate all he did for her.

David and Country A are both perpetrating against a target. We see how an attitude of superiority and entitlement creates adversarial behaviour that is unworkable and oppressive, whether on an international scale between countries or on an interpersonal level between individuals. What is helpful to understand is the similarity of the victimisation *process* underlying different forms of oppression so that the emphasis is taken off the target's reactions and put where it belongs, onto the oppressor.

Links to Other Forms of Abuse

Imagine you have a friend with a superior, entitled, and adversarial attitude. They always act like they're better than you, make all the decisions, and never listen to what you want. It's like they think they're the boss, and you're just there to do what they say.

Now, consider how this attitude plays out in different situations, like when someone is in a cult, captured as a prisoner of war, or is a whistleblower who speaks up about something wrong happening. In these situations, the people in charge believe they are superior and, therefore, entitled to use their power to control and manipulate others, making them feel trapped and powerless. They also use an adversarial approach, meaning they're always ready to argue and fight to keep their power, even if it's unfair.

This same attitude also shows up in bigger groups, like when one race, age group, or gender thinks they're better than others. They use this attitude to put down and mistreat other groups, like with racism or ageism. They're in a constant battle to keep their power over others.

Their attitude creates a power imbalance where one side targets, captures, and traps the other side, making it impossible for them to have equal power or respect, and then blaming the target for their reactions to being treated like that. The adversarial approach means that any attempts to resolve or communicate will be met with all the tactics of Conversational Control. The dynamics are intractable.

A Victim or a Target?

People don't tolerate or permit Conversational Control or Coercive Control. They are trained, groomed, coached, and encouraged by a process common to any form of domination. There is a *process* of victimisation rather than the person being a victim. It is a process of targeting a person with the same attitudinal style and tactics used to destroy the psyche of prisoners of war, or hostages, for example. We can often overlook people's resistance to being targeted and their gradual loss of power, and we fail to see that any resistance can be met with punishment that can be too hard to tolerate. It is a trap.

I often hear, 'Oh, I wouldn't have tolerated that. I would have left/put a stop to it/done better.' I will say, 'That isn't fair, as we are not the ones being subjected to the full range of tactics used on the person you think is merely tolerating that.' We cannot always see or understand the grooming and victimisation process that the target is subjected to.

Most of us have been subjected to a superior, entitled, and adversarial attitudinal style, like when:

- A boss at work acts like they know everything and ignores our ideas, making us feel like we must do things their way,

- An older sibling always gets their way by saying they're in charge and threatening to tell on us if we don't listen,
- A salesperson uses high-pressure tactics, making us feel guilty for not buying something we don't need,
- A friend always insists on picking the restaurant or movie without considering what we want to do.

In all these situations, the person with the superior attitude uses tactics like ignoring our opinions, making threats, or making us feel guilty in order to make us give in and do what they want. It's like they're weaving a web around us that's hard to escape.

Cults

As a young person, I was fascinated by cults and how they operated. I often fantasised that I would never be caught out like that and reckoned that I could resist the pull of a cult culture. That is until I found myself in one, a group that met several times a year, and then tried to extract myself!

The contempt and blaming of me by the cult leader and members was extraordinary. It was then that I understood how easy it is to fall for someone's sense of superiority and an adversarial approach to our resistance, especially when they are meeting a need on some level. I thought my cult was about personal development. However, all I was really doing was accommodating the cult leaders' idea of personal development at the expense of my emotional safety and without learning any viable skills. It was an emotionally abusive, dishonest practice, and I had to withstand the vitriol I experienced when I left.

Luckily for me, I had the support to do that, and this cult could not really continue to affect my life. The effects of being emotionally abused, though, took a long time to resolve and come to terms with. Especially as in those days, not so much was known about emotional abuse. It could be confused with a variation of 'tough love' and 'straight talk', which was, in fact, injurious and not in the least helpful.

Coercive Control is a Process

Typical tactics and behaviours used by those who dominate others make abuse hard to disentangle. Yet we often focus on the personality and attributes of the person dominated or country colonised rather than on what was done to them and how. The victimisation process is entirely overlooked when we focus on the person or country targeted. Yet this is the most important thing. Personality or other attributes are irrelevant if there isn't a level playing field. It is the process being used to make the playing field unfair and unequal that is critical.

It is important to remember that in a Level 4 relationship (refer back to Chapter 4) where one partner uses Coercive Control, they do not so much converse as use a cleverly arranged pattern of Arcing Up and Down to ensure their target complies with and accommodates them. They will always downplay their offending, have a self-focused attitude, and fail to appreciate the balance of power they have or had over their partner. They will not respond with compassion and integrity and will remain wilfully blind to what they are doing.

Their incompetence and misconduct in the relationship will be attributed to their partner, not their failure to evolve a conversation or the relationship to a deeper, safer, and healthier level. A Coercive Controller decides what is discussable and what is not discussable, and will punish and retaliate against you if you overstep the mark. How they do this will depend on what they know about you that will hurt you the most.

Agendas to Keep an Eye Out For

So, we know that the victimisation process can be gradual and grooming, and we are all able to come under the influence of others at some stage of our lives. What can be helpful is to realise that a victimisation process is usually fed by certain agendas.

Lundy Bancroft's work really helped me to think along these lines (see Resources at the end of this book). There are similarities and differences between the styles of tactics used because different people emphasise one or more of these agendas.

The difference between people who use Coercive Control can be which of the following agendas they 'specialise in' or are fixated on. I believe that people who use Coercive Control use all these agendas to some degree, as they interrelate and interlock with one another due to the superior, entitled, and adversarial attitudinal style. Depending on their personality, though, they might be fixated upon one or several of the following agendas to a higher degree. I'll explain ten of them I have observed over my career and repeatedly see.

Diagram 13 - Agendas

It is important to note that we will see these agendas play out in all levels of Conversational Control, but in Level 3 and Level 4, they are consistent and destructive, preventing a true relationship or Relational Justice. Of course, all the agendas do is direct any attempts at conversation, negotiation, or a healthy relationship away from the Middle Column. Whatever agenda they are running at the time will influence the pattern of Arcing Up and Down.

1. I Focus on You Agenda

The 'I Focus on You' agenda comes across as a fixation on defining and describing you without any awareness that this can be a two-way process. You will be met with an adversarial approach if you define them back. It can feel relentless, like you are under the microscope and being policed. It is as if they have accorded themselves the right to decide what is okay and what isn't, but whoever is in partnership with them doesn't have that right. Everything is about *you*, and they will not self-reflect on what they are like in a relationship or on their impact. The signature Double Standard is 'It is my right to decide what is abusive and what isn't,' and the signature Double Bind is 'I destroy your calm then call you crazy.'

I have counselled elderly couples where the male partner was unable to see how he relentlessly fixated on what the female partner was doing or not doing, and whether he approved or whether he would criticise. There was virtually no other conversation. It was shocking to see how this pattern had evolved over the decades of their relationship. In one case, a woman had become so used to it that it took a tradesperson who came to the house to fix something to point it out and beg her to get support. Her husband's communication was substandard, and his attitudinal style was superior, entitled, and adversarial, but he was receptive to recognising that his approach to the relationship was unacceptable. It took a concerted effort on my behalf, though, to point it all out, and the threat that his wife would leave him if he didn't stop, which would have left him alone to manage his physical frailties. His wife, as a result, felt more empowered and knew her rights, and she had family support, so he could not successfully resort to his old ways if he wanted his wife to stay around.

2. Poor Me Agenda

The 'Poor Me' agenda comes into play to keep you catering and accommodating when you challenge them. It works well. When someone you have been afraid to raise an issue with suddenly bursts into tears or seems to fall apart, it takes a super person to refuse to buy into the agenda. The trouble with this agenda is that no matter the level of Conversational Control, the controller can only see where they feel like a victim and how they have been so badly hurt in the past. They will refuse to see how they have mistreated you and are victimising you, or are making you accept Double Standards and Double Binds. Or, it can play out as a sulking attitude and behaviour for hours or days so that you will cater to them. The signature Double Standard is that only they can be the victim, you can't. The signature Double Bind is 'When you challenge me, you are just like everyone else who has mistreated me.'

3. Psychobabble Agenda

The 'Psychobabble' agenda is used by a Coercive Controller wishing to promote themselves as a sensitive, easily hurt person who talks about their 'feelings'. This agenda intends to analyse and dissect you and your motivations, childhood, or personality as punishment for not playing by their rules and somehow 'hurting' their feelings. It cleverly keeps you busy wondering if they are right instead of recognising that they are playing you and skilfully deflecting attention away from the actual issue, which is their behaviour. You are tied up trying to understand what they are saying, but it doesn't make sense and takes you away from your rights and the Middle Column. The signature Double Standard is, 'Nothing is more important than my feelings,' and the signature Double Bind is, 'I assault you psychologically and emotionally and then analyse what your responses say about you.'

4. I Have a Bigger Problem than You Do Agenda

The 'I Have a Bigger Problem Than You Do' agenda is where you are kept in line, accommodating, and catering so you don't trigger their mental health issues or addictions, physical illnesses, or whatever their 'bigger' problem is. Any threat of feeling 'misunderstood' will result in it being your fault if they are triggered into a reaction or relapse. The trouble is, anything will be used as an excuse for a 'trigger', and we get controlled by trying not to 'set them off'.

There is a signature Double Standard of 'I am the one who has to have their problems understood,' and 'Whatever problems that you have or that this creates for you are unwelcome.' We are Double Bound by the notion that if you challenge them, even gently, you are considered mean and totally responsible for the consequences of their reactions or relapse.

5. Don't Inconvenience Me Agenda

The 'Don't Inconvenience Me' Agenda is based on the signature Double Standard that the relationship or conversation should be convenient to them, but they are not concerned about whether it is convenient to you. No matter what normal relationship needs, wants, or requests you have, this agenda means you won't be able to have them properly addressed. The signature Double Bind will be that your normal needs will be treated as inconveniences that you will be condemned for having. This agenda can force you into accepting behaviour you don't want in a relationship because you don't want to be seen as an inconvenience and too difficult.

6. You Are Always Wrong Agenda

The 'You Are Always Wrong' agenda is common in our adversarial world. It can be an attitude as much as the words used to convey that your thoughts, ideas, opinions, and perceptions are inferior and can't be taken seriously. You have no influence on the other person, and there's no response like, 'That's a good point,' or 'I hadn't thought of that.' A signature Double Standard is 'With my intelligence I can't take your opinions seriously,' and the signature Double Bind is that if you disagree or think differently, it means you are not thinking well and are also being disrespectful.

7. My Needs are all I am Concerned With Agenda

When this agenda underlies a relationship, it means you end up revolving around their needs and demands. The signature Double Standard is that their needs are paramount, and the signature Double Bind is that you should be more than grateful if they meet the most basic of their responsibilities to you.

8. I Have the Right to Control Your Schedule and Activities Agenda

This agenda is where you are trained to do things their way, in their time, and on their schedule. The whole family can be trained to operate like an army camp. No one would dare to cross the line as the consequences are terrifying. The signature Double Standard is that only they know how things should be done. The signature Double Bind is that they make it too difficult to stick to their control and will punish you for being unable to do so.

9. Stay in Line Agenda

The 'Stay in Line' agenda is intimidating. You are to stay under their thumb, rule, and decisions or else. The 'or else' can be physical violence, or any form of punishment if they consider that you have disobeyed. The signature Double Standard lies in an assumption of authority. They've positioned themselves as your boss, dictating terms while exempting themselves from the same standards. The signature Double Bind arises from their willingness to treat you unfairly and inflict harm whenever you voice objections, trapping you in a no-win situation where speaking up leads to punishment.

10. Be Scared of Me Agenda

This agenda is also intimidating. It is where you are up against someone who will not just intimidate you; they will threaten and terrify you. It is a dangerous agenda and can be seen operating when Coercive Controllers try to gain and maintain their power over you. The threats can be veiled or very clear as to what will happen should you disobey or try to defy or leave them. The signature Double Standard is that you will have no right to defy or leave them. They will decide when this relationship is over, not you. The signature Double Bind is that they will threaten and frighten you every time you try to be your own person, but also insist you are never good enough.

What to Expect in the Different Levels of Conversational Control

At lower levels of Conversational Control, the tangle of themes, agendas, and Unfair Conversational Tactics are easier to tease out as there is not a strong, thick, impenetrable pattern being woven around you. In Level 1, we might see a few themes and agendas and the odd Conversational Control tactic happening from time to time. In Level 2, some agendas, themes and tactics might arise in a few issues, but there isn't such a level of fear so much as annoyance.

In Level 3, there too many unresolvable issues because of a reliance on themes, agendas and Unfair Conversational Tactics, making the relationship unfair and unequal-most likely abusive.

In Level 4, what may have started as a 'relationship' has become a complex, impenetrable arrangement of themes, agendas and Unfair Conversational Tactics to make use of the target.

These agendas also underlie colonising attitudes and add up to a very incapacitating approach to a country and its culture, or to a partner. It is too hard to keep track of all these agendas, but we can learn to sniff them out over time as we become better at 'playing tennis' with a professional, world-class opponent who has no qualms about beating us.

The costs of higher levels of Conversational Control where these agendas are being played out are enormous for our health and well-being. The lack of a Middle Column builds up, accumulates, and eventually ruins any relationship. There is only so much a person can tolerate before it affects our mind, body, and spirit. It is abusive for someone to expect you to normalise abnormal and unfair communication or to consent to repeatedly coming off as second best. Where there is Coercive Control, an intricate array of Unfair Conversational Tactics, themes, and agendas are used to gain and maintain complete control over you. Physical violence may or may not be just one of the tools used, but as you can see, there are many other aspects that, as a society, we need to understand.

Karly's partner never used physical violence. But he expected her to tolerate and consent to his attitudinal and behavioural style. He expected her to be okay with him controlling the parameters of discussions and how he framed their issues. Her decline in her health and well-being was, in his opinion, a manifestation of either her own poor mental health or something else that was wrong with her. This is a classic example of being interpersonally colonised. There is an obvious inability and interest in a higher level of human interaction.

Instead of collaboration and teamwork, there is warfare. But when a relationship feels like a war, it is no longer a relationship. Some people are too fixated on and fanatical about 'winning'. They act like the arbiter (someone with supreme knowledge and authority) of their partner and the relationship.

At higher levels of Conversational Control, a person shows a lack of interest or insight into what's available in the Middle Column and the possibilities it can bring. We can call it a variety of names, such as narcissistic, controlling, or toxic, but knowing what that actually means and what will happen in the nuts and bolts of the relationship makes it real and down to earth. This allows us to make sense of what is happening, and that it isn't our fault.

This diagram sums it all up.

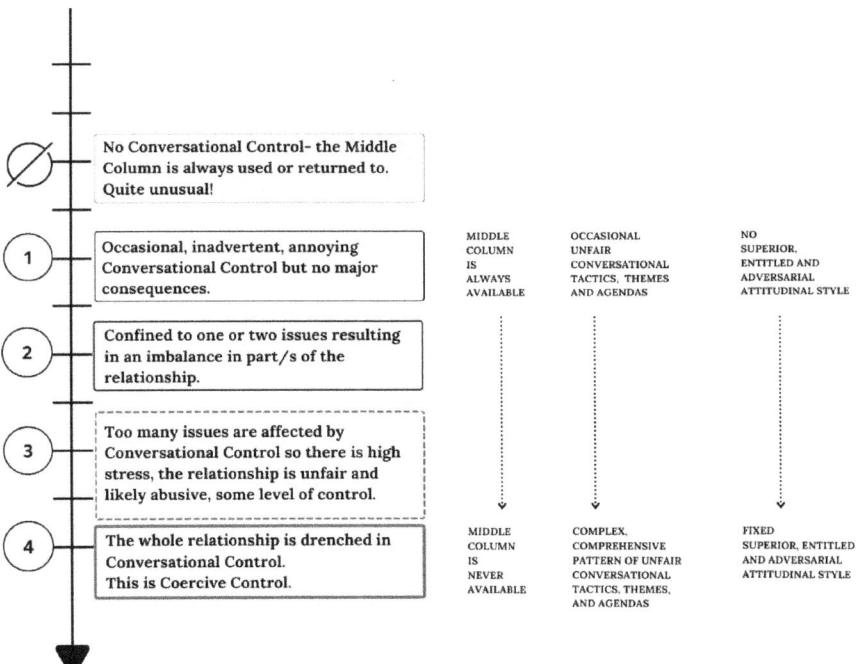

Diagram 14 - The Levels of Conversational Control

9

Why does this matter?

Now you have read this book, you will likely feel more confident in understanding your Conversational Rights, spotting Unfair Conversational Tactics, and recognising conversations promoting or hindering Relational Justice. I also hope you can better identify when conversations are balanced or if they are veering away from the Middle Column, and you are empowered use the framework and phrases in this book to navigate conversations effectively.

Having the clarity and skills to make sense of and decide what to do about any confusing or deceptive language you encounter is a life-changing skill. Words and conversations can get very tangled. Not having the language to articulate why we find certain relationships and conversational styles more difficult is disempowering. However, once you know how to disentangle words and join all the dots, you can express what is happening and how your Conversational Rights are being disrespected.

Once educated, we will all be less vulnerable to Conversational Control and better equipped to teach our children their rights. Sometimes, understanding our Conversational Rights makes all the difference in whether it is possible to be Conversationally Controlled.

Conversational Control is a universal aspect of human interaction across cultures, genders, and contexts. It can be observed in personal relationships, workplaces, communities, and larger societal structures. Humans naturally seek to influence and persuade others, and

Conversational Control is a tool to achieve these ends. It manifests differently depending on cultural norms and individual personalities, but the underlying mechanism of seeking to control or dominate through conversation is present across all human interactions. The mechanics of domination are similar, no matter the context.

So, understanding Conversational Control is crucial for recognising abusive behaviour and promoting healthy communication patterns in all types of relationships, whether personal, professional, societal, or global. This book has highlighted how important it is to be aware of the wide range of Conversational Tactics that can be used to control us in any relationship. As one of my clients, said, 'It's the same dog but just a different leg action.'

Arcing Down tactics might seem insignificant, but as a pattern and in certain conversations, they are serious, cowardly tactics as they turn away from you and leave you high and dry. They are used to compel you to meet their needs and to forget your own.

The tactics in the Arcing Up column will bury the truth and are another form of cowardice. Rather than turning away from you, these tactics are actively turning against you. They are more intimidating and tend to accuse and shift blame. No matter which Unfair Conversational Tactics are used and how they are switched between, they are conversationally irresponsible and Relationally Unjust.

A relationship of any kind requires conversational manners and conversational responsibility to be equal and fair. The Middle Column must be regularly used to maintain connection and trust. Anything else is a betrayal of what a relationship is about, especially if there is a wilful blindness to the consequences and effects.

Using the Framework

For people in relationships where Conversational Control is at lower levels, such as occasional and irritating as in Level 1, or confined to an issue or a few issues as in Level 2, there may be great potential for improvement using the principles of Conversational Equality and Conversational Rights and redirecting old habits of Conversational Control to the Middle Column.

However, if a relationship is further along the continuum, such as Level 3, there is likely a more stressful undertone with longstanding unresolved issues. These may be due to a lack of skills and awareness more than a desire for control, but the attitudinal style towards the relationship has to be checked. If there is a superior, entitled, and adversarial style, change can be difficult, if not impossible.

Level 3 is very common and can resemble a Level 4 relationship, but even though there is a high level of Conversational Control, there is less interest in telling you what you can or can't do, say, think, feel, wear, or eat as in Level 4. Nonetheless, the relationship is still unviable and more of an arrangement that suits the limitations of the person using Conversational Control. It isn't a fair relationship where both people benefit. There may be potential to make changes, but seeking knowledgeable, professional intervention will be safer.

In this case, it is very helpful to have the language to explain how the conversations go, what Unfair Conversational Tactics are being used and how these impact the relationship. This can help our sanity and reduce our confusion, so it is easier to look at the relationship through the lens of Conversational Control rather than the lens of confusion and self-doubt. If you seek help, you have the language to prevent someone from trying to play the victim or complicate matters with a list of complaints about you.

This does not mean you can't try out the framework or phrases if you think your relationship could be at Level 3, but it does mean expecting some retaliation, such as some serious Arcing Up tactics that you will have to feel safe with and know you can manage. You might start by just noticing and then introducing some phrases that you feel okay with, but this will be to keep your sanity rather than make any permanent changes to the relationship's health. It depends on how fixed their attitudinal style is and what themes and agendas underlie their Conversational Control.

It is a Level 4 relationship when one partner uses Conversational Control to prevent their partner from having any input at all into how the relationship is run. There is a fixed superior, entitled, and adversarial attitudinal style, which means that they will decide who makes what decisions, and absolutely no Middle Column is possible; the relationship is dangerously unsafe, unviable, and abusive. *This is Coercive Control.*

Despite the level of control over what you are allowed to do in your life, there may be no incidents of physical abuse, even though you might fear the possibility of that happening. But someone in this situation needs help. Again, understanding how conversations should go, and what Conversational Control is, will give you the language to describe to yourself and others what is happening. It will help keep you saner and give you the clarity and skills to understand the relationship's dynamics. This is especially the case if you are with someone who uses a quieter, less obvious style of Coercive Control.

The Consequences of Conversational Control and Coercive Control

The extent of the problem with Conversational Control, and the reason why this concept matters so much, is that there is such a wide range of physical, emotional, social, sexual, and financial effects and losses for those affected, especially where there is a pattern of abuse. The higher the level of Conversational Control in a relationship, for example, the stronger the mechanics of domination being used that are common to all forms of abuse.

Conversational Control is foundational to all forms of abuse when humans overpower one another. It is foundational to Coercive Control. We need to understand it.

Confusion is Disempowering

One of the most critical responses to Conversational Control is confusion. When we are confused about what is happening, we are more vulnerable to self-doubt and susceptible to Conversational Control. This results in major cumulative losses and effects across all areas of our lives.

Karly said, 'I spent years overwhelmed and unsure of what had happened and whether my expectations in the relationship were too much or whether I had a right just to walk away from that relationship, that maybe things weren't that bad. I just wasn't happy. Now, though, I think things were horrible, and I wouldn't want to live with someone like that again. It wasn't my fault. It wasn't about me at all. How can a relationship happen without decent conversations? But it's taken years to work that out. That was a huge weight I carried all that time that kept me depressed and guilty.'

Being persistently confused like Karly undermines us and easily leads to:

- a gradual loss of confidence
- increased self-doubt and self-blame
- a loss of self
- a sense of dying or fading away
- emotional distress
- loss of trust
- inferiority and feelings of failure
- self-doubt and self-blame
- a sense we are barely surviving
- a deep fear that can be unconscious

It can also lead to:

- a loss of physical health
- anxiety
- depression
- hypervigilance

- tension
- inability to sleep
- suicidal ideation
- nervous breakdowns
- blackouts
- exhaustion

As well as the emotional and physical consequences, there are multiple losses:

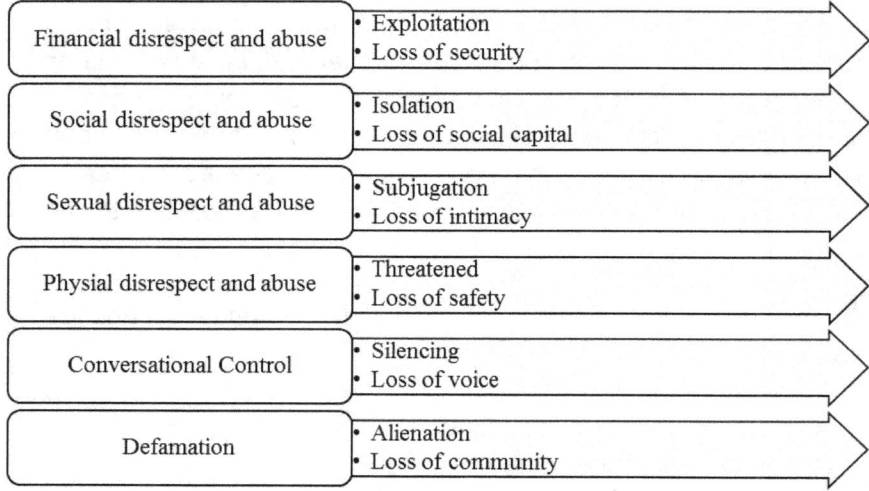

Diagram 15 - Consequences and Losses

Understanding your Conversational Rights, when you have Conversational Equality and when you are being Conversationally Controlled, will lessen the slippery slope that Karly experienced into poor health and well-being, depression, and anxiety. These concepts can help people retain their sense of dignity and reduce the intensity of the feelings of self-blame and confusion that flattened Karly and took her years to recover from.

It's crucial to understand that the Response Framework outlined in this book may not work to redirect conversations in relationships with higher levels of Conversational Control, or where there is Coercive Control. Using any of the responses could worsen the situation as perpetrators of Coercive Control will perceive it through their lens as if you are challenging their authority over you, arousing their suspicion that you need to be retaliated against to be pulled back into line. This can put you in danger. Always be cautious of your safety and call the hotlines listed at the back of this book if you are feeling unsafe.

However, many relationships are able to be repaired. Once both Sarah and Mark understood Conversational Control, how to stay in the Middle Column, and what would happen if they didn't, they had a framework to help them and to role-model for their children. The way they were talking or not talking about issues was also going to be something the children watched and were affected by. Mark was open to change, but Sarah now recognised the tactics and her right to refuse to cater or submit. It was bumpy, but they now had a better understanding of what was happening. It was a level of Conversational Control that was very damaging and created a Relationally Unjust relationship. However, Mark was willing to rearrange himself for a better family life. It remains to be seen if Mark can maintain that willingness and address the harm that he caused to Sarah and the children, but understanding Conversational Control has given them a second chance to at least avoid the post-separation pattern of Conversation Control and/or Coercive Control that will otherwise happen.

There is no doubt that the effects of Conversational Control in intimate relationships, or any relationship with a high level of interdependence, are extensive and serious. Remember, though, that even the occasional Conversational Control typical of Level 1 (or refusal to use the Middle Column) can accumulate over time if never addressed. A Level 1 or 2 of Conversational Control can gradually tilt a relationship over into one where there is less Relational Justice than is needed to make a relationship work.

Ignoring Conversational Equality and Conversational Rights

Neglecting the principles of Conversational Equality, Conversational Rights, and Conversational Control casts a long shadow over personal and societal dynamics. Not only does it affect personal and professional relationships, but it also heightens social tensions as the voices of power are given priority, marginalising others. This breeds resentment and provokes social unrest as marginalised groups have to demand inclusion and respect. Ignoring these principles creates discrimination and oppression between nations, hindering any progress towards a more just and stable world. How can we grow if we don't use these principles to address complex personal, societal, and global challenges?

This book, *Tangled Web of Words*, shows how conversations can control or connect us. On the one hand, it's essential information for people seeking to make sense of a past or current relationship, or concerned about entering a new one. On the other hand, it's a call to action to raise awareness about how understanding Conversational Control is essential for those invested in upholding human rights, such as practitioners and professionals working with or for people. We have a responsibility not only to understand the nuances of control, right down to how the conversations happen in any relationship, but also to role model to our younger generations what is needed for healthy, equal relationships, more just societies, and a safer world.

Acknowledgements

This book stands as a testament to the love and dedication I hold for my two children, Bonnie and Elo. You are both the light of my life and a constant source of inspiration. Bonnie, your exceptional talent with words and your warm, articulate nature continually moves me.

Eloise, your dedication, wisdom, and insight that you brought into our work and discussions together on Conversational Control and Coercive Control have been crucial to my ability to develop and fine-tune the information in this book. Thank you both for your unwavering support and for enriching my understanding of the power of conversations.

I have many other people to thank for their role in the creation of this book:

Firstly, my heartfelt thanks to all my research participants and clients over the last two decades. Your generous sharing of experiences has been invaluable in developing my theories of Coercive Control and Conversational Control.

My gratitude goes to the exceptional academic and practitioner researchers whose hard work, both before and after the 1970s, laid the foundation for my understanding, research, teaching, and counselling in these fields. Discovering Dr. Evan Stark's seminal book, 'Coercive Control: How Men Entrap Women in Personal Life' (2009), was a pivotal moment for me, particularly as he is a social worker. Similarly, Lundy Bancroft's 'Why Does He Do That: Inside the Minds of Angry and Controlling Men' (2002) has been an invaluable resource in my research. More recently, Dr. Emma Katz has highlighted how Coercive Control affects women and children, and the challenges within current legal practices.

To all the researchers, practitioners, journalists, and individuals with lived experience who have tirelessly written, worked, and agitated to bring the dynamics, effects, and consequences of Family Violence and Coercive Control to public attention, I also extend my heartfelt thanks.

To my wonderful friend, ally and mentor, Dr Sharon Thomas, thank you for all the years of your unwavering support, for encouraging me to pursue university studies, and for your expert guidance in all my work.

To all my dear friends, who have supported me for years through the challenging times in this field, as well as through all my research, practice, and personal conundrums—where would I be without you all? You all know who you are.

To my family:

My mother, Else Marie Birkeland, for always believing in me.

My father, Ralph Pitman, for insisting I go to university when I had other plans.

My sister, Lise Pitman, for always keeping me grounded.

My aunts, Catie Pitman and Julia Zimmerman, for being there whenever I needed emotional or academic support, which was often!

To my external supervisor, Angela Powell, who suggested that I write a book accessible to both practitioners and clients, thank you for your invaluable warmth, wisdom and advice.

To my writing team:

My writing mentor and structural editor, Leeza Baric, thank you so much for your generous guidance as well as keeping me on track, which is not for the faint hearted. I could not have completed this book without your expert help and wisdom. Ina Kuhfuss, thank you for the most beautiful cover and design you created for this book. Poppy Solomon, your meticulous attention to the editing process was so reassuring and invaluable. Thank you so much. Also, to the formatters at Polgarus Studio for making the book look professional.

Finally, to you, the reader, who may be seeking to untangle the web of words that has ensnared you, thank you for picking up and reading this book. I hope it provides the clarity and support you need.

'When we speak, we are afraid our words will not be heard nor welcomed, but when we are silent we are still afraid, so it is better to speak.' (Audre Lord)

Work with Torna

Connect with Dr Torna:

Website: https://www.talkingwise.com/

Email: torna@talkingwise.com

Facebook: https://www.facebook.com/TalkingWise

Diagrams and Worksheets

Master Diagram

This is a more detailed version of the Three Columns Diagram found in Chapter 3.

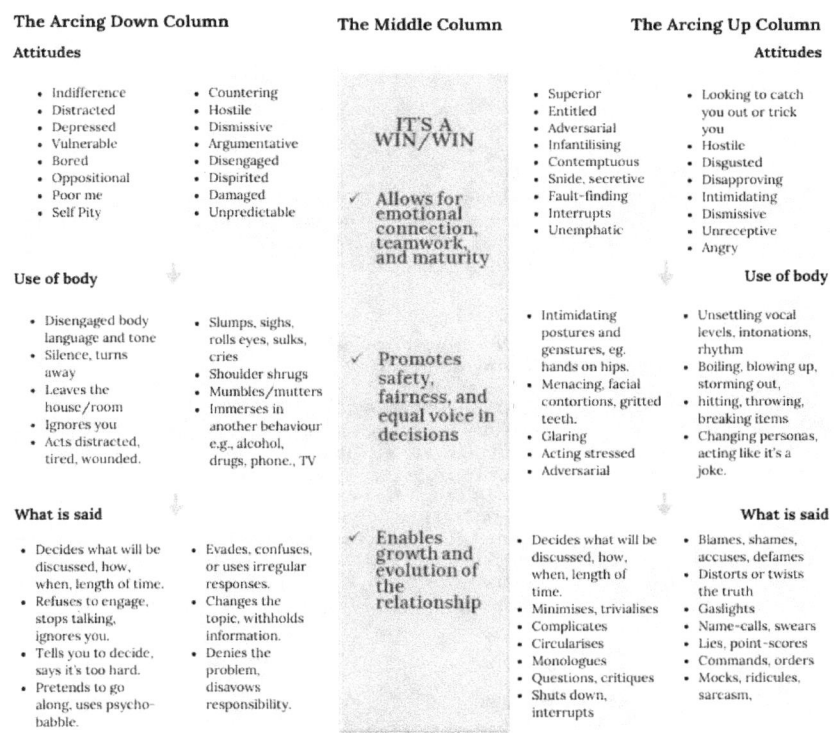

The Arcing Down Column

Attitudes

- Indifference
- Distracted
- Depressed
- Vulnerable
- Bored
- Oppositional
- Poor me
- Self Pity

- Countering
- Hostile
- Dismissive
- Argumentative
- Disengaged
- Dispirited
- Damaged
- Unpredictable

Use of body

- Disengaged body language and tone
- Silence, turns away
- Leaves the house/room
- Ignores you
- Acts distracted, tired, wounded.

- Slumps, sighs, rolls eyes, sulks, cries
- Shoulder shrugs
- Mumbles/mutters
- Immerses in another behaviour e.g., alcohol, drugs, phone., TV

What is said

- Decides what will be discussed, how, when, length of time.
- Refuses to engage, stops talking, ignores you.
- Tells you to decide, says it's too hard.
- Pretends to go along, uses psycho-babble.

- Evades, confuses, or uses irregular responses.
- Changes the topic, withholds information.
- Denies the problem, disavows responsibility.

The Middle Column

IT'S A WIN/WIN

✓ Allows for emotional connection, teamwork, and maturity

✓ Promotes safety, fairness, and equal voice in decisions

✓ Enables growth and evolution of the relationship

The Arcing Up Column

Attitudes

- Superior
- Entitled
- Adversarial
- Infantilising
- Contemptuous
- Snide, secretive
- Fault-finding
- Interrupts
- Unemphatic

- Looking to catch you out or trick you
- Hostile
- Disgusted
- Disapproving
- Intimidating
- Dismissive
- Unreceptive
- Angry

Use of body

- Intimidating postures and genstures, eg. hands on hips.
- Menacing, facial contortions, gritted teeth.
- Glaring
- Acting stressed
- Adversarial

- Unsettling vocal levels, intonations, rhythm
- Boiling, blowing up, storming out,
- hitting, throwing, breaking items
- Changing personas, acting like it's a joke.

What is said

- Decides what will be discussed, how, when, length of time.
- Minimises, trivialises
- Complicates
- Circularises
- Monologues
- Questions, critiques
- Shuts down, interrupts

- Blames, shames, accuses, defames
- Distorts or twists the truth
- Gaslights
- Name-calls, swears
- Lies, point-scores
- Commands, orders
- Mocks, ridicules, sarcasm,

Diagram 16 – Master Diagram of the 3 Columns

3 Step Process for Mapping Conversations and their Consequences

I recommend replicating the following diagrams on paper or on a whiteboard to map out the conversations in a relationship you are concerned about.

Step 1

This diagram can be used as a guide for Step 1, which is to map the conversations in a relationship. Ask yourself or the other person how the conversations tend to go in each area of the relationship. Consider how the dot points in the centre of the diagram apply to the conversations experienced.

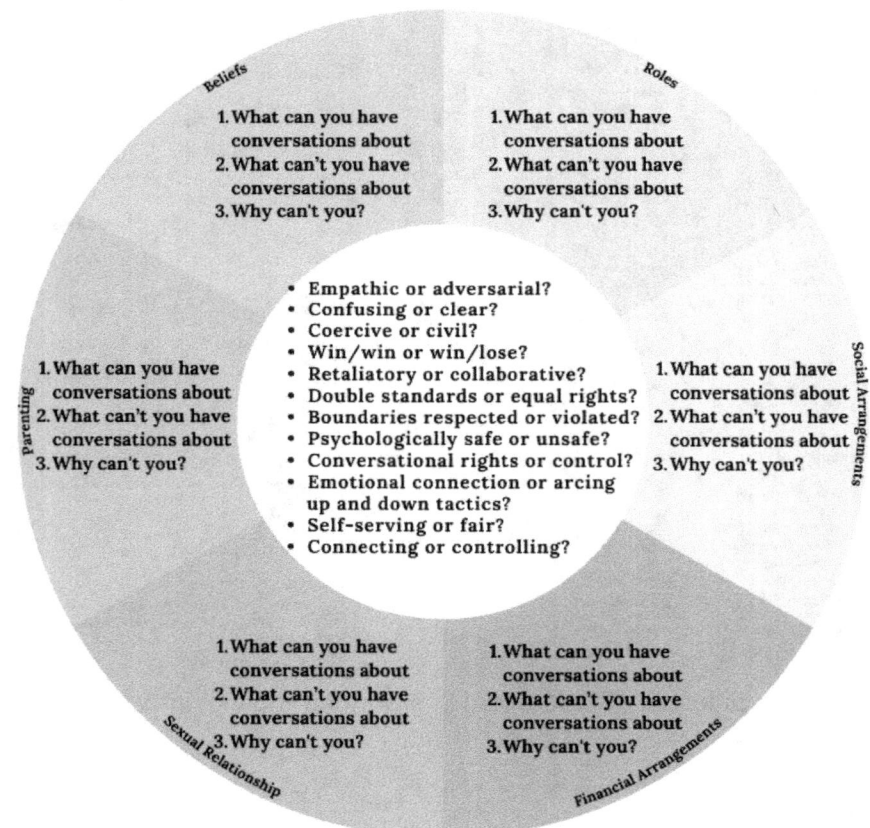

Diagram 17 – Mapping Conversations

TANGLED WEB OF WORDS

Below is an example of how a completed diagram might look.

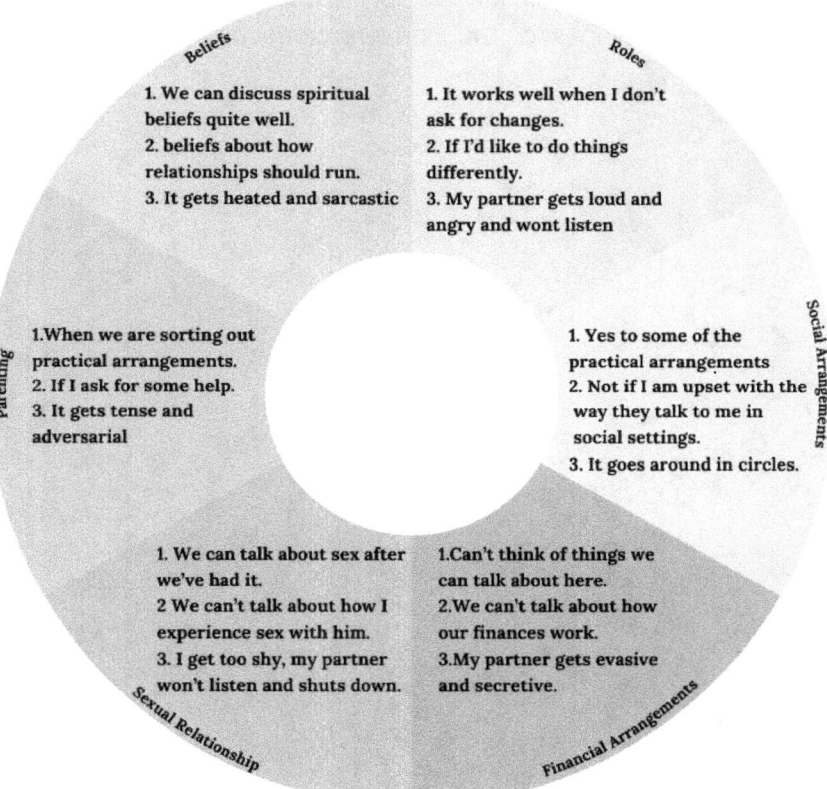

Diagram 18 - Mapping the Conversations - Completed

Step 2

This diagram gives you an idea of how to do Step 2, which is to work out the consequences of the conversations in each area of the relationship.

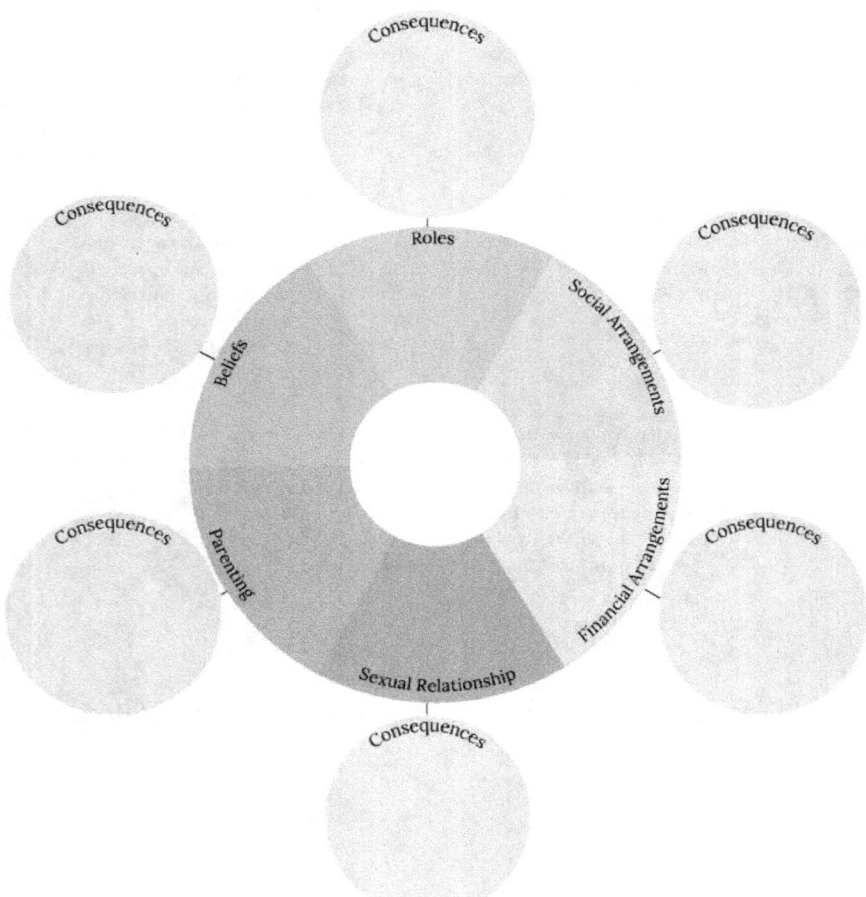

Diagram 19 - The Consequences of Conversational Control

TANGLED WEB OF WORDS

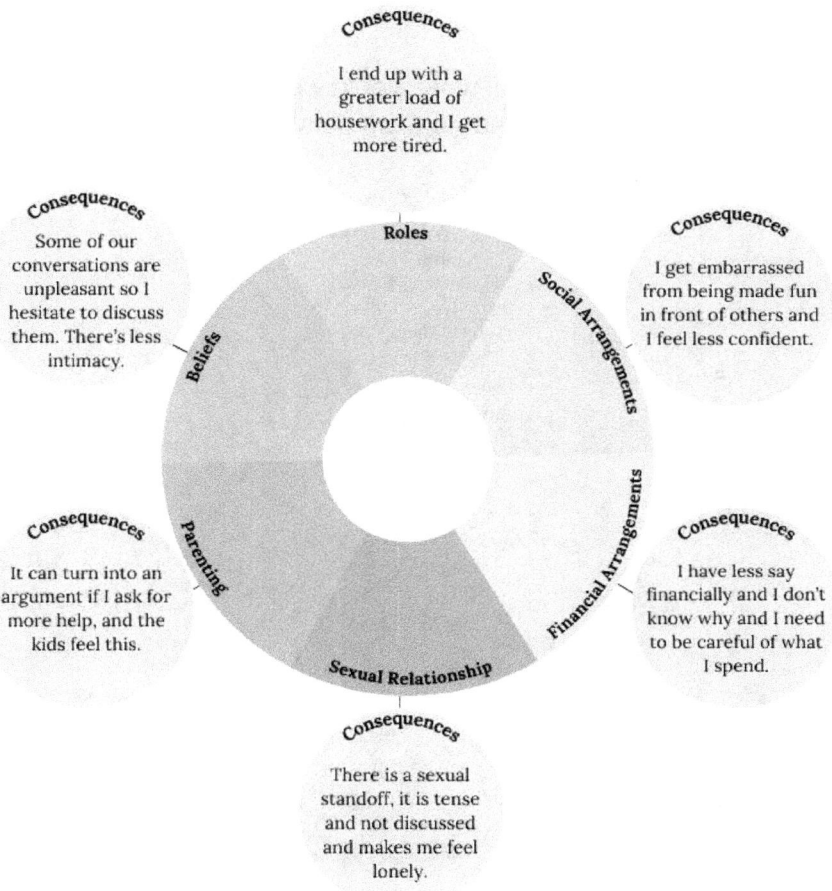

Diagram 20 - Mapping the Consequences

Step 3

The next step is to work out what would work better for you instead. This worksheet gives you some examples to use as a guide.

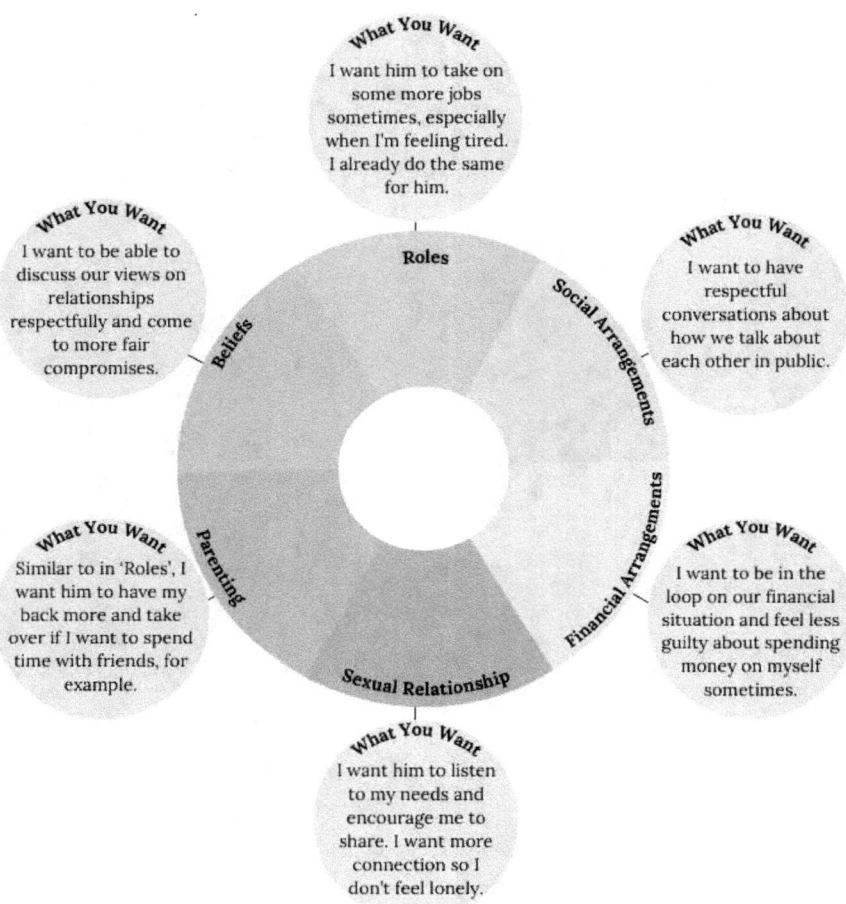

Diagram 21 - Mapping What you Want

Resources

Bancroft, L. (2002). *Why does he do that? Inside the minds of angry and controlling men.* New York: G.P. Putnam and Sons

Bancroft outlines ten possible presentations of Coercive Control. He covers the effects of men who use coercive control on children. He also addresses the problem of trying to separate from a man who uses Coercive Control and what is likely to happen to the women and children post-separation. Lundy is an author, workshop leader, and consultant on domestic abuse and child maltreatment.

Pitman, T. (2010). *The legacy of domestic violence: how the dynamics of abuse continue beyond separation.* University of Tasmania. Doctoral Dissertation, University of Tasmania. https://figshare.utas.edu.au/articles/thesis/The_legacy_of_domestic_violence_how_the_dynamics_of_abuse_continue_beyond_separation/23210972/1

Pitman, T. (2017). Living with Coercive Control: Trapped within a Complex Web of Double Standards, Double Binds and Boundary Violations: *British Journal of Social Work* https://doi.org/10.1093/bjsw/bcw002

Pitman, T. (2022). Coercive Control. Thursday Thoughtcasts. 10-Part Video Series on Coercive Control: https://www.youtube.com/watch?v=ei7Uhtf8w7Q&list=PLXrH0IW0vtxrc4TD4rzlNu89UWxE3Jvzo

Stark, Evan. (2009). *Coercive Control: How men entrap women in personal life.* New York: Oxford University Press.

The Criminalisation of Coercive Control in the UK is based on Stark's work. Stark, a social worker, clearly outlines the way women's experiences at the hands of men in intimate relationships are not captured by the violence model, leaving women and children vulnerable to pre-separation control as well as post-separation control

Herman, Judith. (1997). Trauma and Recovery. Complex Post Traumatic Stress Disorder

CPTSD is often mistaken for personality disorders. Judith Lewis Herman is an American psychiatrist, researcher, teacher, and author focused on understanding and treating incest and traumatic stress. She was one of the first researchers to describe domestic violence as one of the causes of Complex Post Traumatic Stress Disorder.

Walker, Pete. (2013). *Complex PTSD From Surviving to Thriving: A Guide and Map for Recovering from Childhood Trauma.* Azure Coyote, Layfayette, CA.

Pete Walker is a licensed Marriage and Family psychotherapist with degrees in Social Work and Counseling Psychology. Pete Walker added the 'Fawn' trauma reaction to the well-known Fight Flight Freeze trauma reactions. Visit www.PeteWalker.com

Australian Helplines

1800 RESPECT 1800 737 732
1800respect.org.au

LIFELINE 13 11 14
lifeline.org.au

KIDS HELP LINE 1800 551 800
kidshelpline.com.au

ELDER ABUSE HELP LINE 1800 353 374

MEN'S REFERRAL SERVICE 1300 766 491
ntv.org.au

IN AN EMERGENCY SITUATION, ALWAYS CALL 000

Bibliography

Bancroft, L. (2002). *Why does he do that? Inside the minds of angry and controlling men*. New York: G.P. Putnam and Sons

Flood, Michael, Dragiewicz, Molly, & Pease, Bob. (2018). Resistance and backlash to gender equality: An evidence review. Crime and Justice Research Centre, Queensland University of Technology, Brisbane, Qld.

Pitman, T. (2017). Living with Coercive Control: Trapped within a Complex Web of Double Standards, Double Binds and Boundary Violations: *British Journal of Social Work*.
Accessible at https://doi.org/10.1093/bjsw/bcw002

Pitman, T. (2010). *The legacy of domestic violence: how the dynamics of abuse continue beyond separation.* University of Tasmania. Doctoral Dissertation, University of Tasmania.
https://figshare.utas.edu.au/articles/thesis/The_legacy_of_domestic_violence_how_the_dynamics_of_abuse_continue_beyond_separation/23210972/1

www.ingramcontent.com/pod-product-compliance
Lightning Source LLC
Chambersburg PA
CBHW072007290426
44109CB00018B/2164